100 INSTANT FAITH SHARING TALKS

100
Instant Faith
Sharing Talks

IAN KNOX

KINGSWAY PUBLICATIONS
EASTBOURNE

ISBN 0 85476 646 4

Designed and produced by Bookprint Creative Services
P.O. Box 827, BN21 3YJ, England for
KINGSWAY PUBLICATIONS LTD
Lottbridge Drove, Eastbourne, E. Sussex BN23 6NT.
Printed in Great Britain.

This book is a 'thank-you' to Neville Knox (my dad),
Billy Graham and Stephen Olford,
the three greatest influences on my preaching;
and to my wife, Ruth—my greatest encourager.

Contents

Introduction

Who wants to share their faith? The answer is—most Christians do, if only . . . .

If only we knew what to say, and how and when to say it. It is bad enough in a one-to-one situation, with all the inherent dangers of a tricky question or an argumentative friend. But when it comes to having to speak in public, even with half a dozen hearers, we freeze with horror. Not only does the ordinary, average, shy Christian feel like this; many pastors and teachers feel out of their depth when faced with the prospect of speaking evangelistically.

We all have areas of our lives where we feel less than adequate. I have been speaking evangelistically for over thirty-five years, but I experience the same knee-knocking whenever I am asked to do some teaching, or, even worse, pastoring. I need all the help and advice I can get.

Fear not! Help is at hand. It is worth remembering, for example, that the word 'evangelism' comes from the old word 'evangel' which simply means 'good news'. To speak 'evangelistically' thus means talking about the good news and, in days when most news is bad, that has got to be a wonderful thing to do.

But how do we do it? When? What do we say? To

whom? This book seeks to answer these questions. It is written to take the panic out of giving a faith-sharing talk. Here are 100 tried and tested talks which should fit most situations. From private conversation to public platform, from a pub 'do' to a formal dinner, from a children's chat to a bereavement service, you will find something in this book for every occasion, and the two extensive indices will help you find the right talk.

As I have put this book together, my prayer has been, and is, that God will enable you to share your faith in a very meaningful way, so that people may meet Jesus by the power of the Holy Spirit, and reach out to others in their turn.

I am so grateful to Ruth, Sue and Julie for all their help in getting this book together. Thank you, too, to those great speakers, preachers and evangelists who helped to mould my own ministry.

Ian Knox
January 1997

PART 1 – THE TIPS

'Can you fix my car?' the man asked the garage mechanic. 'And can you do it cheaply? I'm a poor preacher.'

'I know you are,' the mechanic replied. 'I heard you last Sunday!'

True or apocryphal, the encounter sums up many people's feelings about those of us who get up to speak about our faith: we are not very good at it. Steve Chalke, one of Britain's most popular preachers, has said, 'The truth is that the modern sermon is not working.' This book is not aiming to defend sermons, but rather to encourage and help those who want to share their faith.

We live in the age of the fifteen second sound-bite. There should be no place in our churches or meetings for boredom, for antiquated styles and language, or for a dull delivery that fails to communicate the good news of Jesus Christ. We have the best-ever news for needy, lost, sinful, helpless and hopeless lives. In sharing our faith with others we can help them to a personal relationship with God through Jesus. The first words ever preached by Jesus were: 'The time has come. The kingdom of God is near. Repent and believe the good news' (Mark 1:15). We want to follow his example, to obey his command and to let him do what he promised—to make us 'fishers of men'.

Why do we do it?

My family, my friends, my neighbours, my area, my land, my world—they all need Jesus urgently, and I have discovered that, when I do share my faith, many people want to hear. They are not out to get me, or laugh at me; they are hungry for the news I have. The words of Jesus in John 4:35 are true today: 'Do you not say, "Four months more and then the harvest"? I tell you, open your eyes and look at the fields! They are ripe for harvest.' When we stand up to share our faith, people want to know the Jesus we talk about. They long for his forgiveness, his new life and the power of the Holy Spirit. They are eager for a personal relationship with God, even if it takes all they have got. This is harvest time!

Evangelists have a gift from God to faith-share (Ephesians 4:11). As with any gift from the Holy Spirit, the gift of evangelism must be used wisely and responsibly. Alas, it is sometimes not, but this is no excuse for the church not calling on evangelists to be part of the life and work of the church. It is the highest calling when someone is allowed by God to stand at the door and invite those on the outside to come into the kingdom. As someone once said, 'God had one Son, and he made him a preacher.'

It may be that you say, 'I'm not sure I have the gift of being an evangelist.' For all such, Paul's final words to Timothy are an encouragement: 'Do the work of an evangelist' (2 Timothy 4:5). We can work at it, and share our faith with God's help. The very definition of a Christian is to confess with our lips as well as to believe in our hearts (Romans 10:9).

As Pope Paul VI put it in his remarkable 'Evangelii Nuntiandi' in 1975, 'It is unthinkable that a person should accept the Word and give himself to the Kingdom without becoming a person who bears witness to it and proclaims it in his turn.' He echoes another Paul, whose cry rings down the centuries, 'Woe to me if I do not preach the Gospel!' (1 Corinthians 9:16).

A major part of faith-sharing will often be with those in need of one kind or another. A social worker said to me, 'We have no aims any more. We have nothing to live for.' People are lost, and purposeless. There is often the darkness of suffering, pain or bereavement. Lives fall apart when marriages fail, or children leave. Sin does spoil, and soil, and there is a yearning to escape from this prison. These are the ones with whom we will share the good news of Jesus, as we show people, not only where they come from, but the potential of what, and whom, they can become in Christ. God's forgiveness brings new life, with its new relationship with the Father, and a new sense of direction and fulfilment.

How do we do it?

Of all the great preachers I have ever heard, none outranks Dr Stephen Olford, who says, 'The keys to effective evangelism are wet eyes, bent knees and a broken heart.' In a similar vein, Billy Graham claims that the three elements of evangelism are, 'Prayer, prayer and prayer.' As we pray, we let Jesus soak our minds with his thoughts and wishes. We need no less than this, and have been promised: 'We have the mind of Christ' (1 Corinthians 2:16).

As we help others into God's kingdom, our lives should reflect his life, so the cry of 'hypocrite' will not be heard as we share his good news. Which is why Alfredo Smith comments, 'We do not need to ask God to anoint our words, but to anoint our lives that we may speak his words.'

Paul tells Timothy, 'Do your best to present yourself to God as one approved, a workman who does not need to be ashamed and who correctly handles the word of truth' (2

Timothy 2:15). This will involve our spiritual lifetime as the background to our words. However, some of the best faith-sharers are those who have known Jesus for a very short time. When Philip brought his friend Nathaniel, he had only met Jesus himself twenty-four hours earlier. A new disciple started with the most simple of invitations, 'Come and see' (John 1:46).

The story is told of David Hume, the eighteenth-century British deistic philosopher, who rejected historic Christianity. He was met by a friend as he hurried along a London street. 'Where are you going?' his friend asked. 'To hear George Whitefield preach.' 'You don't believe what Whitefield preaches, do you?' to which Hume gave the stunning answer, 'No I don't—but he does.' How can we expect anyone to believe what we do not? If God's word has not entered our hearts, why should anyone else take it from us? At the National Evangelical Anglican Congress in 1988, the then Archbishop of Canterbury, Robert Runcie, was the principal guest speaker. In an outstanding address, he quoted Dr Tillich who, when preaching, was asked by a man brandishing a Bible, 'Do you believe this is the word of God?' Tillich replied, 'When you hold it, I'm not so sure. But when it holds you, I know it is.' We discover the power of God's word when we preach it with conviction.

And what about our audience? Do we believe in them, too? Does our heart go out to them with the compassion of Jesus, seeing them as needing a shepherd (Matthew 9:36)? As Archbishop George Carey puts it, 'True evangelism springs out of love.' Our aim is to know the people whom we wish to introduce to Jesus. As we do, we will not see them as 'souls to be saved' but, rather, as real people whom Jesus will make whole.

By now most of us are feeling woefully inadequate! And that is good, for then we will have to rely completely on the Holy Spirit for his wisdom, words and power. After all, we want people to trust God, not us. God is the one who speaks, as Jesus is uplifted, and draws all to himself (John 12:32). To quote Pope Paul VI again, from his '*Evangelii Nuntiandi*', 'Techniques of evangelisation are good, but even the most advanced ones could not replace the gentle action of the Spirit. The most perfect preparation of the evangeliser has no effect without the Holy Spirit. Without the Holy Spirit, the most convincing dialectic has no power over the heart of man.'

Whatever else we do, we must begin with God's Spirit moving our thoughts and words. Whenever I share my faith, be the gathering tiny or huge, I always pray these words before I stand up: 'Fill me, Jesus, fill me now. Fill me, Jesus, with your precious, holy power. I am yours, dear Lord, to do with as you will: so fill me, Jesus, right now.'

What do we say?

The Times newspaper, a year or two ago, carried an extended correspondence on the subject of preaching. One contributor said how he played 'sermon cricket' in his school chapel services. Every time the preacher mentioned himself, he scored a run, while 'God' was a wicket. One sermon ended up 93 for 2!

Prebendary John Collins says that the gospel has not been preached unless the message includes: God, sin, Christ, repentance and faith. Bishop Gavin Reid says that the message must be 'Jesus-centred', and people must be made to feel that 'the issues are too important to ignore'. John Stott, in his book *Christian Mission in a Modern World*, says succinctly, 'In a single word, God's good news is Jesus.' Billy Graham says that he seeks to include in every sermon each of the following: the fact of sin, the cross, the resurrection, the need to repent, faith, obedience, the cost, and then the call to commitment.

That's quite a list, and it is clear that no talk can cover every point fully. So, better to take one aspect and major on it, including some of the other points in passing. Although different talks will deal with some of these points more than others, a faith-sharing talk will almost always end with a call to commitment. We will consider this in more detail in a moment, but we do need to give people the opportunity to say 'Yes' to the call by and claims of Jesus.

The preparation

So, an invitation has come from the Ladies Bright Hour, or the church young people's group or the Rotary Club. Maybe you feel the morning congregation needs to hear how they can meet Jesus, or a local pub wants some carols and a Christmas 'thought'. What are you going to say? The germ-seed of a theme is absolutely essential. The key to all you say lies here.

Now is the time for long thinking and praying (many a good talk will come from a quiet soak in the bath!). We should let the seed idea roll round in our minds, with an A4 piece of lined paper on hand to jot down any and every thought which surfaces. I blitz a rough pad till it looks like a dog's-dinner: an outline, headings, quotes, Bible verses, anecdotes, illustrations and jokes. Then I find it helpful to write out the talk as fully as necessary, transferring my A4 sheet into a couple of pages of script. I edit and re-edit before writing out the notes I will use to speak from. It does take nerve not to speak from a word-for-word script, but a talk which is read is no substitute for a more open delivery.

What is needed is an easily visible set of headings and notes with the main points. Quotes and Bible verses can be in full. Notes should be a maximum of A5 size, on two or three pages at most. They can be hand-written or typed:

the main thing is to be able to read them! White space will help, as will the underlining (or highlighting) of vital points. I always leave a margin for last minute additions, which may arise just before I get up to speak. I never write on both sides: the back of my notes is reserved for the date and place where I gave the talk; an ultimate embarrassment is giving the same talk twice in one place!

The opening remarks

I get an idea for an opening, but tend to play an extremely dangerous game, working out my first words just before I get up to speak. This gives me the chance to pick up on something immediately in the minds of my audience—the latest news, a sports headline, or even something which has happened while we have been in the meeting. From this I can link into the talk, making it have an instant 'now' interest. This can be very effective, but needs considerable nerve: which is why a prepared opening should be available as a fall-back.

A good story, or a personal anecdote, helps as an introduction, as long as it leads into what we have to say in the body of the talk. A wholly irrelevant joke may be the only thing people remember! In truth, it will be us, as much as what we are saying, that people will notice at this early stage. Our clothing, our smile (or nervous twitch!), our looking at (or away from) our hearers, even having our hands in our pockets, will probably say more than the words themselves. Good opening words, and a good impression, will make things go well. Conversely, a hesitant 'umming' and 'err-ing', and a diffident approach, will spoil so much. We need to pray that, from the word 'Go', we come across well. The introduction may take nearly as long to get right as the whole of the rest of the talk.

Illustrating your talk

As this book will demonstrate, I am a great collector of
quotable quotes. There are some excellent books of quota-
tions on the market, but my best quotes book is the one
which I have been compiling for thirty years, because
every quote in it is one which matters to me. I grab other
people's thoughts wherever I go. In church, I scribble on
the service sheet. When David MacInnes came to preach,
he began by apologising to the choir, sitting behind him:
'Excuse my back.' Turning to the congregation, he then
added, 'Excuse my front.' Irresistible as an opening, and
one to remember when you need to get the whole place on
your side.

A good starter is vital, or the audience will have
switched off before they switch on. Get going well. An
up-to-the-minute story, a little anecdote, or a great verse
from the Bible will each help to grab the audience from
the very beginning. On many occasions we are at a minus
position, as they settle into an uncomfortable pew, wonder
how their bottoms will survive, and worry whether the
oven was set right for the roast not to be burnt! We have to
win the right for them even to listen to us.

Using the Bible

If you plan to use a Bible verse or two, a simple reading of
it may be a real turn-off. A little enthusiasm can transform
the situation: 'I have just been reading one of the ultimate
bits of the best book in the world; the book which, last
year, won the Ian Knox "book of the year" award! Listen
to this great quote: "God loved the world so much . . . ."'
Get the idea?

Whatever our theological persuasion, we must beware
of lifting verses out of context in order to prove a point,
completely ignoring their context or historical setting. Use

concordances and commentaries to help you understand the background to a passage.

It's always best to assume that people know nothing about Christianity, even its most basic themes and concepts. If I speak of a Bible character, I give a thumb-nail sketch in two or three sentences ('Zacchaeus—you remember? The tax collector who was too small to see over the crowd, so he climbed a tree to see Jesus coming down the road').

We have to be as simple and straightforward as we can. This does not mean speaking 'down' to our hearers, but it does mean making God's word reach them in an understandable way. Whenever I read my Bible, even in my own private devotions, part of me is looking for a word, a verse, a chapter, with which God will enable me to share my faith in a new talk, or something which will help me to communicate a point more effectively.

Visual aids and illustrations

A picture paints a thousand words, they say. Did anyone do it better than Jesus? Two thousand years later, and with enormous changes in lifestyle, we can immediately visualise many things Jesus said, simply because of the brilliant picture language he used. The merchant looking for fine pearls and finding one he considered perfect, the ten bridesmaids waiting for the bridegroom, the broadcasting of seeds by a sower: each of these is from a bygone age, yet each has a present-day relevance which needs little explanation. We can only guess at the phenomenal impact such pictures had on Jesus' hearers.

Where are our modern equivalents? Are we watching out for simple, helpful ways of getting our message across? In the street and the garden, city centre and countryside, at work and in the media, the pictures we need have already been painted. In this book are visual aids as diverse as a milk bottle, a brick and a road sign. Or think of the new life of a spring flower, the fights on *East-Enders*, the child lost in a crowd.

Those of us who are rather more extrovert need a cautionary note here. With no stories or humour a talk can be dreadfully dull, but a stream of anecdotes, stories and jokes may leave our hearers thinking we are the funniest, wittiest speaker they have ever heard—but they will remember little else. The stories must be our servants, the spices which flavour our faith-sharing so that it becomes tasty.

A small visual aid can be produced at an appropriate moment in a talk. If I am in a church, for example, I will hide my milk bottle, or brick, in the pulpit. Whenever I use acetates, I try to get a real artist to do them for me. With the development of computer graphics and printing, even a complete non-artist can have pictures at the press of a button.

How to deliver the talk

If it were possible to sum up in one word how most people feel about Christian preachers and speakers, that word would be 'boring'. So far, I have attempted to show how the talk itself can avoid this dreadful word. But even the best talk can fall down if we ourselves communicate it badly. The larger-than-life pulpit style may fit a great meeting, but not a coffee morning in someone's front room. A children's talk will need a lot more animation than a bereavement service. However, a kindly style will be effective anywhere, bearing in mind the words of Joseph Parker: 'There is a broken heart in every pew.'

If I am using notes, I make sure there is somewhere to rest them, or I hold them in a small book. In certain circumstances we have to learn our notes off by heart, as they would be a distraction—in a pub, or with lively children, for example. Even with notes we will need to eyeball our audience, and hold their attention. Complicated, lengthy sentences will not help, and technical words need to be unpacked. And if that most dreaded thing of all happens—you lose your place—the rule is: don't panic! As I get older my mind gets worse, and I lose my place more often than I used to. When I do, I own up to it, instead of bluffing it out. 'I have completely forgotten why I was telling that story,' I tell my audience. 'What was I talking about?' I have never known a situation where someone did not call out where I had got to. 'You can come to all my meetings!' I tell my helper. Everyone loves it, and they concentrate as hard as I do from then on.

I had big problems a few years ago. My throat was at the point of packing up. I went to see a speech therapist who was a fellow church member, and Jenny Taylor has given her permission to pass on to others what she told me. Jenny was able to identify three or four reasons why I was struggling. Basically, my throat was having to do too much, and I needed to get everything else working. I had to understand that sound comes, not just from the throat, but from an area covering the top of my nose to way below my Adam's apple. To learn this, Jenny got me to exercise with the letter 'M', which does not come out of the mouth at all (the mouth is shut to say 'M'). I lay in the bath with the exercises (long Ms) Mmmeee, Mmmiii, Mmmmaaaah, and so on. The family loved it, and would break into 'Mmmmeee, Mmmaaah' at most inappropriate moments!

Secondly, there was projection, expelling my voice properly. This involved 'H', shooting out 'Ha, He, Hi, Ho' and so on (another laugh for the family). Then came the explanation that, to project my words, I needed to aim my voice at the back of the meeting, but with a level head (literally). To raise my chin in an attempt to get beyond row one merely stretched my poor throat.

Two more pieces of advice helped. The first was

practising getting lots of breath into my lungs, so the very bottom of my rib cage expanded and my diaphragm extended. It meant pulling air into the lungs till I could take no more, and then keep going! I had to see how many words I could say with one breath. I used months of the year, adding one more with each attempt. In the end, I could reach October in Year 5 before I needed to inhale.

Jenny's final tip was on survival when things were really bad, and speaking could not be avoided. She pointed out that a cold drink was disastrous: cold water does to the throat what a cold shower does to the body—makes it flinch and tighten up. A hot drink flavoured with honey is the answer.

The appeal

In his masterpiece, *The Cross of Christ*, John Stott says that there should be 'no appeal without a proclamation, and no proclamation without an appeal'.

What did he mean? Simply this: if we tell people to become Christians with no substance to our message, that is irresponsible; but if we share our faith and then give no opportunity to respond, that is unfair.

When we consider what the good news is, it becomes inevitable that a decision is demanded by its very nature. The classic definition of a Christian in Romans 10:9–10 is that we should confess Jesus as Lord as well as believing in him in our hearts. John Wesley puts it unequivocally: 'There is no such thing as a private Christian.' If we do not give our hearers the chance to make up their minds at the end of what we say, we fail them. There needs to be a moment of standing up to be counted, and we help that moment to occur.

We are often terrified of this so-called 'head counting', but the fact is, people need to indicate an allegiance to

Jesus Christ. The great curse of Christianity in much of the western world, not least Britain, has been the preponderance of 'secret disciples'. It matters that someone openly responds to Christ.

Some will come to him for forgiveness, others for new life, or hope, or deliverance from sickness or pain: there will be those who need his presence in situations of loneliness or bereavement, while some feel they have to come 'home'. There will often be those who, having once been Christians, feel they have strayed away and are prodigals returning to the Father. Many will be seeking a firm assurance of a faith which, till now, has been too weak to work effectively. The very challenge of being a disciple, with its implicit cost, will cause some to rise and accept it.

They come because the Father draws them, through the quiet voice of the Holy Spirit. Our call, at the end of a faith-sharing talk, is but an echo of that breath of God.

Right up to our present generation, the most expected place for any response to a faith-sharing message was at the front of the meeting, in what was called an 'altar call'. Billy Graham's words echo from his great crusades: 'I'm going to ask you to get up out of your seat.' But there has been a major backing away from this style in recent days, which may not have been helpful for those wishing to make a real commitment to Christ.

I was challenged on this point when visiting a well-known Greater London church to conduct a series of evangelistic meetings. 'How are you going to end your talks?' I was asked by one of the ministers. 'Well, I expect I will ask people to have a quiet word with me after the meetings if they have trusted Christ.' 'We've been doing that for the last ten years,' the minister rejoined, 'and we have ten years of anonymous Christians as a result. We want you to make an open call every time you speak.' With this rebuke, I did as I was asked! In a church of well-to-do, respectable, reserved English men and women, I asked men to stand at breakfast, young people to come out in front of their peers, and Sunday congregations to come to the front of a long, daunting building. Not only did every meeting see great numbers responding, but a second Sunday morning service each week was one lasting result.

Sooner or later, new Christians will have to go 'public'. However hard it seems, it will come best if they do it at the moment of trusting Christ. The whole talk needs to lead up to this moment, so it is not tagged on as a nasty surprise. Counselling should be immediately available in a quiet place, to avoid undue embarrassment. Have we lost a vital element in helping people become Christians by stepping back from the open call? We faith-sharers need to keep this as a major option in our thinking as to where we will call for response.

There are, of course, other ways of helping people to indicate their 'Yes' to Jesus. An enquiry room can be made available for people to go to, which is a slightly easier way of making a public stand with private counsel: counsellors must be ready in the room, or sitting nearby. Cards can be handed out as people arrive, or be on the seats or tables, with various boxes for ticking, but my experience is that most prefer to speak rather than write. We can ask for hands, or heads to be raised, as others pray: but it is hard to find people afterwards to counsel them. Instead of people coming forward, they could remain behind as others leave—but this may be even harder than coming out.

In all my evangelism, I tend to use just two methods of calling for response when it comes to geography. Either I call people forward (or to stand), or I tell them I will be available in a very visible place at the end. I will say something like this: 'I'm going to ask you to do two things. The first is to pray with me right now, silently, as I say the words of a prayer out loud. Then, as soon as the service/meeting/talk is over, I want you to come over to where I am by the door/the bar/that table there. I will have a leaflet which will help you, and we will note your name so we can get you something else. I will understand that your asking for this leaflet says that today you have trusted your life to Christ.' At a dinner party, in a pub, at a home meeting or in a church morning service when people are in a rush to get home to rescue the roast, this method works particularly well. As people come to me, they know that others are watching. But instead of being embarrassed, they are delighted to start out with Christ in this way. All we need is a good leaflet detailing how to begin with Christ, and someone to scribble names and addresses. If counsellors are available, we need to make it clear that someone will chat with them before they go.

In our success-orientated society, it is hard not to feel we have to 'produce the goods'. 'We're hoping for a big response tonight' is a tough thing for a speaker to hear just before a meeting. People have the right to say 'No', and John 6 ends with Jesus allowing many to go away. I often quote my north of England grandmother: 'You're big enough and daft enough to make up your own mind!'

Nor must there be undue emotionalism. I say 'undue', because some emotion may be a good thing. I have seen whole families come forward, as individual people and yet together. As they have stood to publicly profess their faith, they have hugged each other, and it is hard not to weep oneself, seeing their tears of joy. But we are looking for a response which covers the whole person. The mind says yes to Jesus as the truth (John 14:6), the conscience must react positively (2 Corinthians 4:2), as well as the heart (Mark 12:30). If our hearers are not moved by the love of God, as Jesus dies on the cross, they are hardened indeed. But if we get them unnecessarily screwed up, we have got it wrong. As my friend Eric Delve puts it, 'God is not bribing them in, he is dying to get them in.'

The ending

This is the hardest time of all for the speaker. It is an area which needs to be bathed in prayer, as we go through the spiritual battle of bringing people 'from the power of Satan to God' (Acts 26:18). At such a moment of emotional, spiritual and even physical challenge for me, I need to trust God that he will do his work. He is the one who saves.

Be compassionate

It is better for me to be embarrassed than my hearers! If they do not come forward, for example, yelling and screaming will not make it happen. We all have occasions when no one seems to respond: but how do we know what has really happened? At one church service, I gave an invitation for people to come to the front. I stood alone during the entire hymn. I pronounced the benediction, feeling dreadful. Only as folk went home did an elderly lady come up and tell me she should have come. She wept as she told me of a lifetime away from God, and the burden of sin. It was lovely to see her trust Christ. She needed mercy—from my style, as well as from God.

Be clear and courteous

People need to know what they are being asked to do with Christ's call. I was horrified to attend the meeting of a world-renowned, though controversial, American evangelist when he made his 'appeal'. All he asked his vast congregation to do, if they wanted to trust Christ, was to bow their heads and pray. But then he got those who had prayed to stand. Not content with this, he then told them to come to the front of the vast auditorium—and to run as they did! As they stood there, he asked those with drug addiction to raise their hands. Those who did were brought right on to the platform, lined up in rows, and prayed for—but not before his television crew filmed them. I could not believe it: they were asked only to bow their heads in prayer, and ended up being filmed on stage. No wonder evangelism gets a bad name. All that is needed is a clear explanation of how we are about to close our talk, with a complete lack of manipulation. Our hearers will appreciate a simple, kindly, understandable request. Singing a hymn over and over again may prove a real turn-off.

Be cautious

We need to listen to God, giving the Holy Spirit time to do his work. The call should not be rushed, and the natural inhibitions in people recognised. I well remember a lovely village congregation where one or two had come forward. As the hymn proceeded, I could feel the longing, bound by fear, in those who could hardly even sing. With a couple of verses to go, I said a few brief words of encouragement, and then prayed out loud, 'O Lord, release these lovely people from their fear, giving them your courage.' Two thirds came out, as the flood-gates opened. Listening to the Holy Spirit is vital.

Be confident

All through the talk we should be making it clear that we, and God, expect people to respond positively to what the Holy Spirit is saying. At the end, what is the point of, 'Well, maybe, perhaps, you could, if you want to, come forward—or see me afterwards—or go home and think about it'? In that case, don't bother! I would much rather go for, 'God is calling. Trust him now. You come.'

C.H. Spurgeon, that oft-quoted nineteenth-century preacher, was asked by a young evangelist about why no one seemed to respond when he preached. 'Surely you don't expect people to respond every time you preach, do you?' Spurgeon enquired. 'Well, no, not every time,' was the reply. 'That's why they don't,' was Spurgeon's punch-line. I believe in these days people are hungry for God, and I trust there will be those who turn to Christ every time I give a faith-sharing talk. We need to be confident that the Holy Spirit is at work—or why are we getting up to speak in the first place?

Be concerned

There needs to be a proper sense of urgency in our own minds as we encourage people to trust Jesus. When will we ever have another chance to speak, or they to respond? The two men sitting by the roadside outside Jericho in Matthew 20:29–34, did not know it was the last time Jesus would walk that way—but it was.

When we encourage people to trust Christ we are asking them to do three things: to admit their need of him, to believe that he is the answer to that need, and to commit their lives to him, having recognised the cost and challenge of doing so.

I use a simple prayer, which I explain first. I ask people to pray, phrase by phrase, silently, these words: 'Lord Jesus Christ, I give you my whole life now. Please come and live in my heart. Wash away all my sins. Fill me with your Holy Spirit.' Then I pray a prayer of thanks that Christ has received them, and will never let them go. I show them the leaflet I am offering, and then I go straight into the call to stand or come forward as we sing a hymn.

Go for it!

Coventry City, a very fine soccer team, had won nothing for 103 years—in itself quite an achievement! In 1987 they had a song: 'Go for it, go for it, City: Sky Blues, shooting to win.' Whether the song made a great deal of difference is questionable, but they not only reached

Wembley, but beat the mighty Tottenham Hotspur to win the Cup.

I felt no shame in lifting the words 'Go for it' as the title for a video on faith-sharing, which we use in the 40:3 Trust (with whom I work). To every reader of this book, I would say: Go for it! In faith-sharing, D.L. Moody got it right when he said, 'My purpose in life is to go to heaven and take as many people as possible with me.'

Let's go for it!

PART 2 – THE TALKS

1. Your Starter for Ten

As with *University Challenge*, sometimes we need a talk to get us in, to get us going in a difficult situation. It is what some people would call 'pre-evangelism'.

Here are some 'openers', which may provide material for situations such as school assemblies, secular clubs, or where proselytisation is not permitted.

1.1 The Love of God

Bible references: Isaiah 49:15–16; 1 John 4:8–10,19.

Audience: School assemblies, youth groups, open-air meetings.

Aims: To show God's love in Jesus. To help a cynical group think Christianity is OK.

Handy hint: Grab the audience by the throat (metaphorically!) right at the beginning, or you are lost. Keep the talk to 5–7 minutes. Don't push the ending: this is a 'starter', not a talk with a call to respond.

Visual aid: If you have got a tattoo (in a polite place!), you are the perfect visual aid. If not, find a friend who has, and take them along—they don't need to speak, just show!

Outline: Ask if anyone is madly, deeply in love. Talk about someone you know who has a tattoo with a name on it ('Mum', 'Ermintrude', 'Birmingham City')—the love of their life. Move quickly to the Babylonian army taking away the Israeli youth in Isaiah's time, and the mothers getting their hands tattooed with their children's names. They would remember their children every day.

Recall God's strange question, 'Can a mother forget her

child?' Then his answer, that she may forget, leads to 'I won't forget you—I have tattooed you on the palms of my hands.' What is the tattoo like? It's the shape of a Roman nail. God hasn't stayed far away—Jesus has lived and died for us. Point to your palm and say, 'God loves you like that—Jesus was nailed to the cross to pay for our wrong.'

Conclude with a simple question: 'If God loves you that much [pointing to your palms], what are you going to do about it?' Then sit down!

1.2 In Good Heart

Bible references: Isaiah 28:16; Ezekiel 36:22–32; 1 Peter 2:1–10.

Audience: Good for open-air work, children, young people and any time a quick talk is needed.

Aim: To show the fundamental difference Jesus makes: nothing short of a change of heart.

Visual aids: A big rock and a clean brick are both vital.

Handy hint: With big visual aids, make the talk reasonably dramatic, short and to the point. Don't injure anyone!

Outline: Work the talk around Ezekiel 36:26. Produce the rock: describe where you got it (the garden, the moors, a mountain—get an interesting one!). It's not much use. Recall Ezekiel—that is how God pictures our hearts: dead and stony-hard through the wrong things which have spoiled us.

Talk about Jesus, taking our stony sins on the cross, and how they killed him. He took our hearts in his heart, which became a broken heart. As a result, God can take our stony heart away. You could, if you are brave, describe one or two of the ways your heart has been stony, and how Jesus dealt with the situation.

The Ezekiel verse goes on to talk of 'a heart of flesh'. Stick with that if you want. Or you can use Isaiah 28:16 leading to 1 Peter 2:6. A new stone can come to our lives, as Jesus becomes the foundation on which we build: time to produce the brick. Jesus is the cornerstone for a new life, which God gives us. Speak of how this has become true for you, and of the building work in progress.

Even in a 'hands off' situation, you might feel able to end with, 'How about that for you?' Gauge the opportunity carefully in your ending.

1.3 Bureau de Change

Bible reference: Matthew 18:3.

Audience: Open-air meetings; school assemblies; when a 'quickie' is needed.

Aim: To show Jesus is the one who changes lives.

Visual aids: A bank note. A bank note from a country you have visited (the more remote the better).

Outline: Say how proud you are to be British (Irish, American—presumably you know what you are . . .). Produce your national bank note: the best currency, buys anything. Till one day you went to Italy (Kenya, Niger, Thailand) and, horror—they would not accept your money!

You could introduce the parallel here, or after producing *their* money. We think our 'good' lives are fine anywhere, and it is a shock to realise God says, 'Not good enough.'

Your currency needs a change, into—produce the foreign note: that's good there! Jesus came with a new way of living, and a life of eternal value: have your audience got it?

Where did you change your money? At a Bureau de

Change. God has one: Jesus can change our lives (Matthew 18:3), taking the old with his death, rising to make us rich before God.

You could say how that happened for you: and now you can spend that life here, as well as in heaven: it has worldwide standing!

Handy hint: This is a good talk to give in a country where you are not a national, because the story is even more against yourself.

1.4 If only . . .

Bible references: Matthew 10:3; John 11:16; 14:5–7; 20:20–29. The John 20 passage is good if in a preaching situation.

Audience: Doubters. The Sunday after Easter evening congregation.

Aim: To show that, with all our doubts, we can find the answers in Jesus.

Handy hint: Make it a happy talk!

Outline: Is there something you always get wrong? Failed your driving test fifteen times, buy the wrong things at the supermarket, forget names? Admit to doubts in believing in God, too—and what a relief to find someone who always got it wrong when following Jesus.

Introduce our 'hero', Thomas: one of the twelve (Matthew 10:3). He only has four speaking roles, and with every one he says something wrong! He never realises the truth till later. First is when Lazarus dies (research the whole incident in John 11). What a statement of non-faith he makes in John 11:16! Not 'Jesus, go and bring him back to life'—just 'Let's all die!' He doubted that Jesus could deal with what had gone wrong. Say how there

are things in your life that have gone wrong: you have
come to believe Jesus can deal with them. Talk about the
cross: as Thomas found Jesus could say 'Lazarus come
out.'

His second 'speaking part' is in John 14:5–7. Surely
after three years Thomas has confidence in Jesus and the
future? He must know where Jesus is going—mustn't he?
No! Make it sound funny, which it is (and sad, too). Say
how glad you are Thomas doubted, because you love verse
six. Rejoice that Jesus has the future in his hand.

The last two events are the Easter encounters in John
20. How can anyone doubt ten honest friends, all saying
and showing the same thing? Good old Thomas does
(v.25)! Even when he finally gets it right (v.28) he should
have got there sooner (v.29). He doubted the present presence of the risen Lord. Say how the presence of Jesus day
by day changes your life.

Past, future, present, Thomas got it wrong. But—a big
but—in South India today the church carries the name of
its founder, Thomas: the Marthoma church. He travelled
further than anyone when he finally trusted Jesus completely. Will we be like those Jesus speaks of in John
20:29? Challenge your audience, as seems appropriate.

1.5 You Matter

Bible references: Matthew 6:25–34; 10:1–4; 29–30; John 1:12; 3:1; 4:7; 6:9; Galatians 2:20; 1 Timothy 1:15.

Audience: Those who don't think Jesus is for them; school assemblies.

Aim: To show we matter to Jesus.

Handy hint: Show your own delight that what you say is true for you as well as your hearers.

Outline: Bemoan how unimportant we all are. Who cares? Mention how you are a number, not a name, to your bank. Other examples which come to mind might include your old school head who only knew you because you were the worst pupil!

Tell of your amazement when you realised you mattered to the greatest one of all, to God. Who says so? Jesus, God's Son, that's who. Using Matthew 6:25–34 and 10:29–30 as your basis, show how Jesus spoke of the beauty of grass and birds, and us mattering more. Even our hairs are numbered. (Make a passing reference to a balding person—yourself, your husband, the chairperson of the meeting—do it kindly!)

Secondly, you know you matter because we are all like

the very ordinary people Jesus called and spent time with. Pick your favourites and describe them in a sentence or two: the disciples (Matthew 10:1–4), the glorious variety of people in the first half dozen chapters of John, eg Nicodemus (3:1), the Samaritan woman (4:7), the boy with loaves and fishes (6:9). You are glad you are ordinary—those are Jesus' sort of people!

Even with an audience of complete outsiders, the cross will have a real impact. That is your final reason for knowing you matter to God, because Jesus died for you (Galatians 2:20), even if you were the worst (1 Timothy 1:15).

The problem is—will we let ourselves matter? If we do . . . a passing wrap-up with John 1:12 might be good, not as an 'appeal' but as a thought left floating.

2. In From the Cold

With an increasing number of people being almost wholly ignorant of the Christian faith, some talks will need to start from scratch. Here are a few ideas which assume little or no knowledge or faith.

2.1 Is God Real?

Bible references: Genesis 1:1; John 14:6; Romans 5:8; 1 Timothy 2:5.

Audience: Atheists; doubters; sceptics; beginners.

Aim: To prove God.

Handy hint: Don't be cocky! You are trying to help people know God, not show how brilliant a debater you are. Be humble. Remember, the UK figures for 'I believe in God' are always between 74% and 77% every year. A recent opinion poll also asked 'Do you definitely *not* believe in God?' and only 4% said 'Yes'. Most people have a wavering belief, or don't know.

Outline: Why do I believe in God? Admit at the outset it is tough to believe in someone we have never seen. Here are your six reasons. (Don't say you've got six, or they will think you are going to go on for ever!)

Creation

'When I look through a telescope, I know there's a God. When I look through a microscope, I know there's a God' (Billy Graham). Evolution, the Big Bang, the Six Days of Genesis, all say 'How?' The question is, 'Who?'—which

44

Genesis answers: 'God created' (1:1). Show a flower. If it were plastic, it would be made by someone. Say you have never met a plastic flower maker! But, as your flower is real—did no one make it? You have no idea how plastic flowers are made; nor real ones, but both have creators. Speak of the intricate detail, the design. Who did it? God.

Jesus

See the arguments in 'I don't believe in Jesus' (on the next page). Who is he? Clearly, God.

Bible

Whose book is it? Explain that it claims to be 'The word of God': 2,600 times in the Old Testament, 525 in the New, it says things like, 'And God said . . . .' The same lie so often—or the truth? Say how long you have been reading it, and how it speaks to you and convinces you of God.

Others' experience

Say that no tribe has ever been found which did not believe in a god. Are all Jews, Hindus, Muslims also wrong? You are trying to prove God, remember. If you want to show the Christian God is right, refer to John 14:6, 1 Timothy 2:5 and Romans 5:8. Speaking of others, talk of the greatness of humanity. For what? For nothing? You believe in a *purpose of life*: we are created *for* God, as well as by him.

You know him

Finally, get very personal. Give your own testimony as to his reality. It is hard to argue against real experience. Share one or two moments when he has been especially real. Tell your audience that they could know God, too—if they wanted to.

2.2 I Don't Believe in Jesus

Bible references: Mark 4:41; John 7:46; 8:58; 13:1–5; 14:9; Galatians 2:20; 2 Corinthians 5:21.

Audience: Sceptics; those who know little of Christianity.

Aim: To show that Jesus is God.

Outline: Explain that Christianity, more than any other religion, depends on its founder rather than any teaching. The Muslim faith could stand without Mohammed, the Buddhist without Buddha. They would be weakened, but survive. But there is no Christianity without Christ. Who is he? You believe he is God, no less. Why?

You have looked at *his life*. Show what an amazing man he was. Pick your favourite sayings/miracles/moments to demonstrate this (Mark 4:41, John 7:46). Spend some time majoring on *his death*, showing how wonderful it was, how vital and how personal (Galatians 2:20). No other faith has this substitutionary atonement (you could use the remarkable 2 Corinthians 5:21).

Talk about *his resurrection*: how it really happened, one of the most proven events of history. So many witnesses, so many appearances, so many writers. The whole of *history* seems to be *his-story*. Countless millions over

2,000 years have known this Jesus. Speak about your own encounter with him, and the difference he makes in your life. Your own testimony is vital, because you *do* believe in Jesus.

What sort of person was he? There are only four possibilities. Was he *mad*? If so he was a megalomaniac (believed he was great, really he was nuts). John 13:1–5 is excellent here: knowing his greatness, he got his disciples to bow down? No, he washed their feet. He acted the opposite of a power-crazy leader. Jesus was a failed maniac. Was he *bad*? No one believes he was—all his deeds and words were good. He was not deliberately leading people astray. Now explain that the next one is the one most believe: he was *good*. But he claimed to be God (John 8:58, 14:9). That is mad—or bad. But he wasn't those. Yet good people tell the truth: so he had (and has) to be—*God*.

Try not to end on an argumentative note. Rather, speak of the joy of believing in Jesus: the release that faith brings; not faith in a good but unproveable ideal, but in a living, loving Lord.

Handy hint: There are two distinct lines of argument here: you may be best taking one or the other, or taking two talks to cover both.

2.3 Introducing—Jesus!

Bible Reading: Matthew 1:18–25. Also Genesis 3:15; Isaiah 7:14; 9:6; 53:6; Micah 5:2; Luke 19:10; John 1:1, 29; 3:16; 4:14; 6:35.

Audience: Outsiders; Christmas gatherings (in and out of church); new Christians.

Aim: To give an introduction to Jesus, explaining why he came, and how he can be known personally.

Outline: So who *is* this Jesus? Why do Christians make such a big thing of him? If you ever had questions like this, it will make a great opening to say how, and why. If not, have a couple of anecdotes of friends who felt/feel like this.

You would like to introduce your audience to this best friend of yours. Who is he? Mary's son—yes, but the father? Joke about 'it takes two', and how Joseph had a problem. Refer back to Isaiah 7:14 and 9:6, and Micah 5:2, getting to John 1:1 without being too argumentative. Speak of how amazing it is that Jesus is God, visiting us as a real human.

Don't linger too long on that, because you also want to share why he is here. Matthew 1:21 says it is to 'save his people from their sins'. You could even refer back to Genesis 3:15, and the first promise regarding Jesus paying for sin; or look at John the Baptist's prophecy in John 1:29, or Jesus' own testimony in Luke 19:10. Isaiah 53:6 has an 'all' sandwich to explain why Jesus came. Share how Jesus came to save you personally, as well as your hearers.

Talk of people having more than one name. Have you got two or more? Jesus is also 'Immanuel'. 'Jesus' means 'the one who saves'. Say what a great meaning 'Immanuel' has: 'God with us' (Matthew 1:23). You could say how he came to be with ordinary folk—shepherds, wise men, us. His life is like water to be drunk (John 4:14) and bread to be eaten (John 6:35).

If your audience is far out, leave it there. Or give the opportunity to respond: for example, 'I'd like you to meet my friend, now I've told you about him.'

2.4 Christianity? It's Impossible!

Bible references: Isaiah 7:14; Matthew 1:20–21; 4:1–11; Mark 4:41; Luke 1:34–35; 2:52; John 7:46; 8:46; 17:3; Romans 12:1; 1 Corinthians 15:4–8, 45; 1 John 5:11–12.

Audience: Doubters; lawyers; after-dinner speech; young people; men.

Aim: To prove that Christianity is the truth, leading to our being able to trust Christ completely.

Handy hint: With a vast amount of potential things to say, be succinct and keep it moving.

Outline: Start by enthusing about how great Christianity seems: a relationship with God, forgiveness, eternal life, the Holy Spirit's power, and so on. If only it were true! But these Christians say the most impossible things . . . So you intend to grasp the nettle/hot potatoes. What words don't go together to make sense?

Virgin birth

'It takes two, babe' (Marvin Gaye and Kim Weston). Hundreds of years before, it was predicted (Isaiah 7:14), and the Greek (if not the Hebrew) does mean 'virgin'. What was Mary if not a slut? See how matter-of-factly

Matthew and Luke write, and Luke was a doctor (Matthew 1:20–21, Luke 1:34–35). Show how Jesus had to be human to be one of us, yet truly God to bring God to us. He needed a human parent and a God parent.

Perfect man

Jesus grows (Luke 2:52) to be perfect. Now there's a novelty! You could even ask the perfect men to stand. (Vicar: 'Stand up anyone who's perfect.' A little old man gets slowly to his feet. 'I didn't know you were perfect, George.' 'I'm not—I'm standing on behalf of my wife's first husband.') Show how Jesus was a real man—hungry, tired, weeping, enjoying friends, dying. And perfect (Matthew 4:1–11, Mark 4:41, John 7:46, 8:46 are all good here). Which means that, when he died, it could be for our sins, not his: talk about the cross for us.

Empty tomb

'Life—the period between birth and death' (Dictionary), so 'empty tomb' is impossible—except that the evidence proves it (see Outline for 'Conclusive Evidence', Talk 15.3). 1 Corinthians 15:4–8 is good. Which means we can have 'eternal life' because of Jesus (1 Corinthians 15:45, John 17:3, 1 John 5:11–12). Speak of the impact of this on you.

Living sacrifice

This all leads to the huge challenge, to take two final impossibly linked words: 'living sacrifice' (Romans 12:1) In other words, total commitment. Say how impossible this is for you ('sacrifices' are dead!) and how only the Holy Spirit can make it happen. Challenge your audience to make the commitment.

2.5 Well, What Do You Know?

Bible references: Job 19:25; John 9:25; 17:3; 2 Timothy 1:12; 1 John 5:13.

Audience: Open-air meetings; non-proselytisation situations; complete outsiders.

Aim: To speak of how you know God personally.

Handy hint: As this is a form of personal testimony, you should be able to give it anywhere. It is not a 'sermon', merely a personal statement, a witness to what you have found to be true. Make it personal with examples from your life throughout.

Outline: Jokingly admit that some Christians give the impression of not being sure of believing anything these days: mention one or two current bones of contention. Say that you are a Christian and, despite everything, you are sure of at least one or two things.

You know God is real (there is material on this in Talk 2.1). Give two or three reasons which are important in this belief, and say how such a belief does not come easily. You could speak of someone who suffers yet still believes, eg Job, and his great credo in Job 19:25. It really is possible to know God (John 17:3).

Now say that things fell into place when you came to know God personally through Jesus. Talk of your own encounter with him, and how your conversion opened your eyes. Compare the blind man's statement in John 9:25, 'I was blind but now I see!'

As your first meeting with Jesus will have been some time ago, give a couple of instances which bear out, in your life, what Paul says in 2 Timothy 1:12, 'I know whom I have believed . . . he is able to guard.' Now you are sure (1 John 5:13).

Be careful of your limitations, depending on to whom you are speaking. End the talk by pushing the boat out as far as possible, without going too far. Eg 'You could know this, too—I'm not in an exclusive club.' Or 'I'm happy to talk afterwards.' Or 'Here's a booklet—do ask for/take one.'

2.6 What's God Like?

Bible references: Genesis 1:26–27; Exodus 20:4; Psalm 8:4–5; Isaiah 52:14; 55:8–9; Matthew 27:46; John 1:18; 10:30; 14:6, 9, 26; 16:13; Romans 1:19–20, 25; 3:23; 8:29; 2 Corinthians 5:21; Philippians 2:9–11; Colossians 1:15.

Audience: This is a talk which follows a reasoned course, so the hearers need to be fairly intelligent.

Aim: To work through the barriers to knowing God.

Handy hint: In speaking to people who are some way from God, you do not need to quote all your Bible references, giving chapter and verse: simply use and paraphrase as appropriate.

Outline: Start by saying how you wish you could see God and how many people you've met would believe if they could see him.

That is Problem One: 'No one has ever seen God' (John 1:18). How can we? You might refer to Isaiah 55:8–9, and God's command for us not to portray any 'graven image' (Exodus 20:4). The answer is two-fold: God is seen in his creation, as Paul puts it brilliantly in Romans 1:19–20. Secondly, God is seen in humans: we are made in his image (Genesis 1:26–27), 'a little less than God' (Psalm 8:4–5). Then ask, 'Do you see God in creation, and in humans?' Answer: Not often!

That is Problem Two. We have spoiled the image and 'fallen short' (Romans 3:23), changing 'the truth about God for a lie' (Romans 1:25). Speak about our failures and sins taking us from God. Then give the second half of the John 1:18 verse you have already used: Jesus shows us God (also Colossians 1:15). Jesus claimed as much in John 10:30 and 14:9.

Show how Jesus then took our broken image of God (2 Corinthians 5:21), which destroyed his 'image', too (Isaiah 52:14) as he was separated from God (Matthew 27:46), before being restored by God (Philippians 2:9–11). Now he is the way back for us (John 14:6), and he changes us to be as we should always have been (Romans 8:29), teaching (John 14:26) and guiding (John 16:13) us.

What a lot of material! You will have to pick and choose, unless you have a sharp style and a patient audience. At the end, encourage people to come to know God through Jesus, as they trust him.

3. Take a Theme

Simple illustrations and relevant parables worked well for Jesus, so why not use his style today? Here are some modern, everyday themes to enable the hearer to feel at home with what is said.

3.1 Gold!

Bible references: Job 23:10; Psalm 19:7–11; 119:127; Haggai 2:23; Zechariah 13:9; Romans 3:23; 1 Peter 1:17–21; Revelation 3:17–18.

Audience: Almost anyone, anywhere; weddings.

Aim: To show that God wants the very best for our lives, as we give ourselves to him.

Visual aids: You wouldn't have a gold bar, would you? Make do with a gold coin. If you have a gold Blood Donor's book, and a wedding ring, they will help.

Outline: Pick a gold opening to show its importance in everyday life. Eg is your local radio called 'Capital Gold', 'Piccadilly Gold', 'Mercia Gold' or similar? The National Lottery has a gold finger (so does James Bond!). Or show how gold has always meant 'the winner', 'the best'. That is what God wants for our lives—the best. What gold does he bring?

Gold = rich. That is what most people think. Check Revelation 3:17–18, and compare our poverty and God's riches: Romans 3:23 shows how we have fallen. Psalm 19:10 speaks of God's ways being 'more precious than gold', as does Psalm 119:127. We are rich for ever with

God. C.S Lewis said, 'Once a man is united to God, how could he not live for ever? Once a man is separated from God, what can he do but wither and die?'

Gold = pure. In Revelation 3, and in Zechariah 13:9, God speaks of us being 'refined', as gold is made pure. Job 23:10 is a great verse: if you have time, you could talk of Job's courage in saying it.

Gold (here is a strange one!) = life. Blood donors who give fifty donations get a special donor's book: a gold one! Whether or not you use that fact, 1 Peter 1:18–19 is great.

Best of all, gold = mine. That is what gold wedding rings say, and what God says in Haggai 2:23. God wants to use us, as we belong to him. He wants us to be part of him, and to share his life.

Invite a response, as you review each point in conclusion.

3.2 Who Is a Christian?

Bible references: Matthew 10:39; John 6:37; 2 Corinthians 5:17, 21; Colossians 1:27.

Audience: Anyone, but especially good for children, or if you want to explain Christianity very simply.

Aim: To help people give their lives to Christ.

Visual aid: Two milk bottles (you will only use one, but you need a spare in case disaster strikes and you drop the first one!).

Author's note: This has been my most used talk, and I have seen more people trust Jesus with this very simple presentation than any other.

Outline: Open by saying that you would like to show everyone a Christian—and produce the milk bottle: you could even read its name (Co-op). Milk is the fastest thing in the world—past your eyes (pasteurised) before you see it. Threaten to throw the bottle in the nearest river/lake, as you toss it from one hand to the other (practise beforehand!). Straight in to 2 Corinthians 5:17: 'Anyone in Christ is a new creation—the old gone, the new come.'

Share how that happened for you, and why it is so important. *First*: we are safe with Jesus. If we keep our lives, we lose them (Matthew 10:39). *Second*: his hand is different from yours—it has a scar: speak of the cross, and the love with which Jesus receives us, and the certainty of his welcome (John 6:37).

What happens when the bottle hits the water? It fills up! So the bottle is in the water, and the water is in the bottle. Get to Colossians 1:27: 'Christ in you, the hope of glory.' How can we succeed as Christians? Jesus does it for us!

Put in your own stories and illustrations, but end with a real call for people to put their lives in the nail-pierced hand of Jesus—with one final throw of the bottle.

3.3 Me

Bible references: John 1:12; 3:3; 6:37; 10:9, 28; Hebrews 13:5; Revelation 3:20.

Audience: Children; open-air meetings; when a quick talk is needed.

Aim: To show the certainty of a personal relationship with Jesus Christ.

Visual aids: Your birth certificate and passport. A New Testament.

Outline: You are going to talk about yourself. There are one or two things you will reveal, to prove who you are.

Number One: British (or whatever!). Flourish your birth certificate. How much will you read out (especially date of birth!)? Only a piece of paper—all you need to show you are British (American, Irish . . .). You had to be born here to get it.

Number Two: Another piece of paper—hold the page with John 10:9 on it (you can use any other verse which speaks of new birth, becoming a Christian, eg Revelation 3:20, John 1:12, 3:3). Explain what it means, and relate how it is true for you.

A birth certificate = born. John 10:9 (or another) = born into God's kingdom.

Number One gives you a right to *Number Three*: A passport. Dare you show your photo? Flash it before their eyes so they miss it! Say how the Queen (President) has promised to protect you: the first page says so. Maybe it will work . . . but John 10:28 (again, choose a similar verse, which proves the safety Jesus gives, eg Hebrews 13:5, John 6:37). Only a little book (the passport) gives safety, because of whose authority is behind it. And your New Testament—God's Word—gives *Number Four*: Assurance of eternal life—safety for ever.

Say how glad you are to be British, but even more happy to have the life Jesus gives. Ask your audience if they have got the One and Three and Two and Four. It depends how young they are as to how you end; be gentle with small children.

3.4 The Way to Life

Bible references: Jeremiah 21:8; Ezekiel 18:4; Matthew 7:14; 27:51; Luke 2:52; John 8:34; 14:6; Romans 3:23; 5:9; 1 Corinthians 10:13; Philippians 2:5–8; 1 John 1:7; 5:12; Jude 24.

Audience: Children; young people; family services.

Visual aids: Pictures, drawings, acetates of road signs, as indicated in the Outline: The *Highway Code* has the correct versions!

Handy hint: Keep the talk flowing: there are a lot of pictures.

Outline: We are on life's journey. The *school* sign could show this: two people walking. Are we going God's way? The *speed restriction* sign shows there are rules: equate this with God's rules for living. If you have a fast car, the speed rule is boring, but if you get out and walk across the road, the rule may save your life. So it is with God's advice on how to live.

The *skid* sign has a car going backwards (check where the wheels are in relation to the start of the skid). We are going the wrong way, choosing death and not life (Jeremiah 21:8): every one of us (Romans 3:23). *Danger, canal* has a car going into the water. You could bring in John 8:34 and Ezekiel 18:4.

But someone got it right (*one way* sign) even when young (Luke 2:52). To go with Jesus means life (1 John 5:12), with his power (*overhead cables* is an exciting one!). His way is sometimes rough (*bumpy road*)—Matthew 7:14, as he makes us right (Jude 24). The devil makes it tough: you could use *falling rocks* as a light-hearted picture of the devil chucking temptations at us, and then bring in 1 Corinthians 10:13.

How can we get on this Way to Life? The *cross-roads* sign is fairly obvious. Jesus crossed over to us (Philippians 2:5–8), crossed out our sin (Romans 5:9, 1 John 1:7): now he is the way (John 14:6).

As a dramatic ending, you could get a *no U-turn* sign, with the bar detachable, and pull it off to show that we can now turn: Matthew 27:51 may help here. Invite people to come on to Jesus' road.

3.5 The Way of Life

Bible references: Joshua 1:9; Psalm 119:105; Proverbs 3:5–6; Luke 11:13; John 10:16; Acts 1:8; 4:20; 1 Corinthians 12:27; 15:57; Galatians 5:22–23; 6:2; 2 Timothy 1:7; Hebrews 10:25; 13:5; 1 Peter 2:2.

Audience: New Christians, especially those helped by Talk 3.4 on the previous page. The next family service after that talk.

Aim: To show how God wants us to live.

Visual aids: As on 'The Way to Life' (the previous page).

Handy hint: If there is too much for one talk, make it two or three. Pepper the talk with simple stories from your own walk with Jesus—successes *and* failures.

Outline: As this is a follow-up talk to the last one, a couple of the road signs there could be the introduction here: eg the *one way* of Jesus, or the *cross-roads*. You could use the *school* sign to show the journey of life, walking along. Christians are a family, who share life together (Hebrews 10:25) as a body (1 Corinthians 12:27). The *men at work* might help you to talk about the way we work with and for each other (Galatians 6:2).

What about those not on the way yet? There are good road signs to help as visual aids here. Why not have a picture of a sign pointing to your own town? It says a lot by being there: that could lead to Acts 1:8. Speaking about Jesus may be hard, but Acts 4:20 is good. The *road joining this road* sign would encourage a reference to John 10:16. That is what we do for God: what does he do for us on this journey?

He guides us. An *information* sign could lead to 1 Peter 2:2 and God's word to show the way. Don't miss out the assurance of safety in Hebrews 13:5. The information is ongoing: you could use Psalm 119:105, or Proverbs 3:5–6. Secondly, God empowers us. The *overhead cables* can be pulled from the previous talk for Luke 11:13, Galatians 5:22–23, 2 Timothy 1:7 and 1 Corinthians 15:57. There may be enough material in these few verses alone for a complete talk.

The *no stopping* sign is a good one with which to end, coupled with Joshua 1:9.

3.6 The Net

Bible references: Hosea 11:4; John 8:36.

Audience: Anyone; gardeners.

Aim: To take the simplest happening and use it as a parable.

Handy hint: Work out a parallel presentation from your own experience, if this particular story has not happened for you. The aim of this whole section is to show how everyday events can be used in a similar way to the style Jesus formulated in his own parables (a sower, fishing, bridesmaids waiting for a wedding). The incident in this talk is clearly one which will not have happened for many, but it is included to show how a momentary occurrence can lead to an explanation of the gospel which everyone can follow. Because of this, part of the Outline is written in the first person.

Outline: I love gardening! I grow my vegetables from seeds, after painstakingly preparing the ground. I hate losing the new growth, so I net those seeds needing maximum protection. I was enjoying a Saturday morning coffee when my young sons ran up the garden, shouting 'There's a thrush in the lettuces!' I rushed down. The little blighter had got under the net, gorged itself and, in trying to get out the wrong way, had forced its head through the net and was completely stuck.

Murder was the first thought—but not in front of the children! With the secateurs in one hand, and holding the criminal very gently with the other, I cut my net to set it free. Was there gratitude? No—a swivelling head brought a beak onto my hand, making holes in me as I rescued the bird.

Do you get the drift? God gave us a lovely world, which we ruined. As Jesus came to set us free (Hosea 11:4, John 8:36) we cut the hands that saved us. It is time to sing out 'Thank you'. This conclusion can be extemporised and expounded, as time allows.

If you have a fruit cage, and a similar experience, go for it! If not, see how everyday life can give parable pictures.

3.7 The Lifeboat

Bible references: Luke 19:10; Galatians 2:20.

Audience: Anyone; a seaside open-air meeting.

Aim: To show the greatness of God's love, his way of rescuing us, and how that depends on his effort, not ours.

Illustration: A first-hand sighting of a lifeboat will help. Being rescued by one would be perfect!

Outline: Talk of your love of the seaside, your favourite fishing harbour, the lifeboat; how you remember when, last summer, you heard of one lifeboat crew who set out to rescue a dog at the foot of some cliffs (a true story, in the papers). Make something of their courage, and sacrifice, and that they are all volunteers.

Now for the truth behind this parable. Jesus has set out in the storms of life to rescue us from where we are in danger of death from our sins. 'The Son of Man came to seek and to save what was lost' (Luke 19:10). You will probably want to speak of his being a volunteer, and the greatness of his sacrifice: he came in the water and drowned so we could be rescued.

It may also be appropriate to contrast a lifeboat rescue with a helicopter lowering a rope. Many people have an 'I did it my way' image of getting to God, as if he lowers a rope from above and we grab hold, then we haul ourselves up by our own strength. Alas, we keep letting go, and falling back in the water! Instead, God's rescue is lifeboat-style, where Jesus throws us into his craft, and we are safe: 'Not I, but Christ' (Galatians 2:20).

Conclude by asking, 'Who is in the lifeboat?'

3.8 Across a Cross

Bible references: Psalm 81:6; Matthew 11:29; John 10:16; Romans 5:8; 1 Corinthians 1:18–25; 2:1–2; Revelation 1:5.

Audience: With good visuals, almost anyone, including children, family services, open-air meetings, outsiders.

Aim: To explain, very simply, the meaning of the cross.

Visual aids: One good sized cross (able to be held and moved) will do. Or a number of pictures/acetates showing crosses doing the various things described in the Outline ie (1) Upright for the start. (2) Angled—X—for a kiss. (3) The word SIN with an angled cross crossing out the word. (4) Addition and multiplying signs. (5) A box with JESUS, plus an X as a vote for Jesus.

Outline: Using the Corinthians verses as the basis, you are going to answer the question, why is the cross so special? (Hold up/show a cross.) What does a cross mean?

First: the angled cross (X). Get people to call out: hope that they will reply 'Wrong' (as when teachers mark papers). Say what sad people: to you it is a kiss! A cross says, 'I love you' (have a personal example here). Romans 5:8 is God's kiss. Is he weak, and giving in? No, says 1 Corinthians 1:25.

But they were nearly right: a cross does not say 'wrong', but it does cross out wrong: your picture/acetate has SIN crossed out. Pope Paul VI in 1975: 'As the kernel and centre of his Good News, Christ proclaims salvation, this gift of God which is liberation from everything that oppresses man but which is above all liberation from sin and the evil one, in the joy of knowing God.' You could use Revelation 1:5 or Psalm 81:6.

From there to the addition and multiplication signs of the cross: as the 'power of God' (1 Corinthians 1:18), we team up with Jesus to reach others (Matthew 11:29). Bishop Williamson of Southwark: 'We cannot keep silent about the Good News we have been given.' You could bring in John 10:16.

A cross is the way we vote to say 'Yes'. Your visual/acetate of the word JESUS with an X next to it gives you your conclusion, allied to 1 Corinthians 1:21: 'Those who *believe*.' He gave his cross to say 'Yes' to us. Is our X vote for him?

4. Chapter and Verse

Some guidelines to show how a verse or two, or a whole chapter from the Bible, can provide the basis for an outline. After looking at these, have a go at working out a talk from your own favourite Bible verses and chapters.

4.1 The Greatest Sentence in the World

Bible reference: John 3:16.

Audience: Should work in most situations: home, open air, with young and old.

Aim: To show the heart of the good news with a simple word-by-word explanation.

Handy hint: Don't 'preach' this talk. Make it chatty, with good stories and illustrations as you explain the words and build towards the conclusion.

Outline: Claim that you can define Christianity in one sentence: then admit it is not yours! Quote John 3:16. Find a subject you know very little about (eg car repairs, fly-fishing, judo, origami). Take one or two words people use for the subject—and how you need an explanation. You are going to do this with your sentence.

Walk through John 3:16 in order (except for 'whoever believes in him', which you tackle last).

'God'—Creator, holy, all-powerful, perfect: paint a BIG picture, which makes the word 'loved' extra-special. Talk about someone loving you, and how you felt. 'The world': do you live on planet earth? He loves you!

Show the greatness of God's love—'so much'. He did

not lend, 'he gave' (give a good example of the difference) 'his only Son'—all the way to the horrible cross, so that we 'should not perish'. Don't miss the negative: but accentuate the positive of 'everlasting life', including the present tense of 'have'.

Don't make it sound *too* easy: go back to 'whoever believes', and explain commitment to Jesus as Lord. You could speak of your own reaction to the verse: put your own name in place of 'the world' and 'whoever'—it does work! Then ask who will put their name in the verse, as a response to this greatest love in the greatest sentence.

4.2 A Grain of Wheat

Bible reference: John 12:24 (plus vv.25–26).

Audience: Depends on how the subject is handled: could be good for most, including teenagers.

Aim: To show the relevance and vital place of the cross—for Jesus, and in our lives, too.

Visual aid: A single grain of wheat, and a whole ear, will show the contrast. Joke with those at the back that they should have sat nearer to see the former!

Handy hint: In a serious talk like this, don't get too heavy. But don't hide the challenge. Really seek the Holy Spirit's help to get the balance right. If you know *The Voyage of the Dawn Treader* by C.S. Lewis, the story of Eustace as a dragon being set free by Aslan is a good illustration.

Outline: Enthuse about how great it would have been to meet Jesus. He was a tourist attraction. Dramatise the Greeks coming to Philip (Greek name) in John 12:20 with their request (v.21), Philip not knowing what to do and asking Andrew (v.22). What an odd thing for Jesus to

78

say in the verse in question (v.24). What on earth was he talking about?

Now for his parable: he remains alone, unless he dies to pay for our sins. When he does, we can be part of the 'many seeds'. Explain how the cross makes it possible for us to cross back to God. Jesus is a grain of wheat.

And we must be, too. Verse 25 shows how our old lives must die, as we give ourselves to him. You could have a second grain of wheat to hold—and then place it in your other hand as if giving yourself to Jesus: which would pick up the middle of verse 26.

Conclude along the lines of: 'Jesus gave all he had got so we might be part of the seed-time and harvest of his kingdom: dare we give all we've got to him?'

4.3 Burdens

Bible reading: Matthew 11:28–30. Also Philippians 2:6–8.

Audience: Especially appropriate for the elderly, the bereaved, the tired—and country folk, farming communities.

Aim: To show how Jesus comes to share our lives in all their needs.

Visual aid: Could you get hold of a yoke? Or a blown-up photo of oxen ploughing with one? Think creatively!

Outline: Start with a first-hand story of seeing a yoke used: ideal if you have been to a country in Africa or the Indian sub-continent, or similar. At the very least, resort to a yoke seen on TV. Speak of the strength of the team, and the help each is to the other.

Go along the lines of: 'Jesus Christ knows your life— the pressures, and pains. He'd like to team up with you— to help.' Now is the time for those Matthew 11 verses, and a brief explanation of them.

Life is hard. What about a little Shakespeare? 'The slings and arrows of outrageous fortune . . . ' Make it personal, with a couple of examples of yourself being 'weary and burdened', and how much you need God's help.

Bring your audience to that lovely description Jesus gives of himself in the middle of verse 29: you could parallel it with Paul's poetry in Philippians 2:6–8. Speak of Jesus going all the way to the cross—*that* humble.

Now he offers two things. There is a new peace (v.28): peace with God. But this will take us to a new work ('Take my yoke upon you'), as we go with Jesus into the future. He will make it possible ('Learn from me'), and a joy (v.30).

You could end by simply requoting the verses, and asking who will share the yoke of Jesus today.

4.4 What a Life!

Bible reading: Isaiah 55. Also Jeremiah 2:13; Romans 6:23.

Audience: Church congregations; other situations where a whole chapter of the Bible being read would not be out of place.

Aim: To unlock one chapter of the Bible (Isaiah 55) to explain the life God gives.

Handy hint: Watch how the chapter says all you need (ignore the other Bible references if you wish), to enable you to find other passages where your audience can follow a talk in their Bibles without needing to turn a page.

Outline: Ask for your hearers' forgiveness, but you are an enthusiast (others are allowed to be about a sport, a lover, a hobby): you love God's new life in you! People have raved for a long time about this life: 2,500 years ago Isaiah did: get them to listen to chapter 55. Say how you want to pick out your favourite bits. What is life from God like?

It is *great*. The best—wine and milk (v.1), satisfying (v.2), with complete forgiveness for the old life (v.7).

Explain that it is because God is so great (vv.8–9), and gives the best (vv.13–14).

For you, this life is *necessary*: you *are* thirsty (v.1), and you often do go the wrong way (start of v.2, an echo of Jeremiah 2:13). 'Wicked' in verse 7 means us all. That is why Jesus needed to die on the cross.

Ask how you could earn such a life. No way: so it is *free* (v.1), as Paul says in Romans 6:23. Jesus has paid for it, totally. Which means the life is *universal*: 'All' (v.1), for 'wicked' and 'evil' people (v.7). And, because Jesus has bought it, and God gives it, such a life is *sure*. Show that God made covenants (v.3), and he keeps his promises: as sure as the rain! (v.10). We *will* go with joy (v.12). Be sure to show that this is for sharing, too (v.11).

So, what will your hearers do about this life? Because it is *now* (v.6) when we receive it. A final run-through as you pick out the call of God to them: 'Come' (v.1), 'Listen, delight' (v.2), 'Give ear and come to me' (v.3), 'Seek the Lord . . . call on him while he is near' (v.6), 'Turn to the Lord' (v.7). Who will respond?

5. Have a Hymn

Some of the great hymn writers of the past wrote their hymns in order to help unlettered ordinary people remember and take hold of great truths from the word of God. A well-known hymn can provide an excellent basis for a talk. Here are four examples to get you going.

5.1 Rock of Ages

Bible readings: Exodus 33:12–23; 34:5–8; Romans 5:1–11. Also Exodus 3:14; 15:26; Psalm 90:2; Isaiah 53:5; 64:6; Malachi 3:6; Matthew 27:3–5; Mark 2:17; John 5:24; 8:58; 19:34; Romans 3:19; 5:6, 11; 6:23; 13:14; Galatians 2:15–16; Hebrews 9:27; 13:8; 1 John 1:7; 5:19; Revelation 3:17; 20:11.

Audience: Church services; older people.

Aim: To use the hymn 'Rock of Ages' to explain how we need to come to Christ.

Handy hint: Lots of material here: prune, pick and choose the points vital to your conclusion. Of course you will need the service to include 'Rock of Ages'.

Outline: Your introduction could be the eighteenth-century West Country storm, when Augustus Montagu Toplady sheltered in the crevice of a huge rock in Burrington Coombe, and the words of the hymn 'Rock of Ages' were formed, as he pictured himself hiding in Christ from life's storms.

Explain how God is the changeless Rock, as life around us shifts (Malachi 3:6), the eternal 'I am' (Exodus 3:14, John 8:58), everlasting (Psalm 90:2, Hebrews 13:8). In him is safety, 'Rock of Ages' (a name not in the Bible, Toplady's idea).

Talk about how this rock was broken, because of our sin: 'Of sin the double cure' (Mark 2:17). We are in sin's 'power' (1 John 5:19), 'naked' (Revelation 3:17), 'helpless' (Romans 5:6), 'foul' (Isaiah 64:6), 'guilty' (Romans 3:19), under 'judgement' (Hebrews 9:27), and going to 'die' (Romans 6:23). (You will find each quoted word in the hymn.) Muhammad Ali (boxer) said, 'I'm scared of no one. I'm only scared of death.'

Now show how Toplady points, throughout the hymn, to the answer in Jesus. 'Cleft for me' (Isaiah 53:5)—speak of the cross. The 'water and the blood'—a broken heart (John 19:34), gives a 'double cure' (Exodus 15:26), will 'cleanse me' (1 John 1:7), and 'atone' (Romans 5:11 AV 'We have atonement' ie 'at-one-ment'). We receive 'dress' (Romans 13:14), and eternal protection at the 'judgement throne' (Revelation 20:11, but see John 5:24). Say how we all need this: who knows when? (Toplady died aged thirty-eight.)

Ask your hearers if their song is, 'I did it my way'— 'The labours of my hands'—and take them to the end of that verse in the hymn, and Galatians 2:15–16. 'Tears' are not enough (Judas, in Matthew 27:3–5).

You could end with Moses' request (Exodus 33:18), and God's beautiful response in verse 22, coupled with 'Rock of Ages . . . let *me* hide *myself* in *Thee*': invite your hearers to say that, now.

5.2 Freedom Road

Bible reading: Romans 5:1–11. Also 2 Timothy 4:8.

Audience: Songs of praise; churches which sing old hymns; Methodists.

Aim: To show the way to God, using a hymn and a Bible passage.

Illustration: You will need the words of Charles Wesley's hymn 'And can it be' in books or on sheets of paper for everyone either to look at as you speak, or, at least, to sing before or (better) after.

Handy hint: A little knowledge of Charles Wesley would help (a couple of facts are in the Outline).

Outline: You could start by saying how you love Wesley's hymns. Or you could lament how others can express the Christian faith better than you, so you intend to get help from one who has done that: Charles Wesley.
'And can it be', written in 1738 (one of 8,000+ hymns Wesley wrote), is a journey on Freedom Road. Explain the two beginnings. Jesus left 'His Father's throne above'. Share something of the greatness of Jesus, 'Very God of very God' (Nicene Creed).

Now the huge contrast: we are 'Fast *bound* in sin and nature's night'; 'Long my *imprisoned* spirit lay'; 'Part of Adam's *helpless* race'; Under '*condemnation*'. You could bring in Romans 5:8, 10, 6 and 9 for each line. Who is like this? Wesley says he was. A wicked man? No: a Church of England rector for three years, a missionary to Georgia (USA), a Methodist at the 'Holy Club' at Oxford University, all prior to his conversion in May 1738. Speak of your own need of Jesus as he came for you.

So to the meeting: pick out from the hymn such references as 'bled for Adam's helpless race', 'Died he for me . . . Amazing love', to show Jesus coming to die to set us free. Get to 'My chains fell off, my heart was free', echoed by Wesley speaking of 20th May 1738: 'I gave myself up to Christ.'

Freedom Road is here! 'I rose, went forth and followed Thee.' Speak from the hymn and your own experience of the new life, as you and Wesley come 'Alive in him . . . clothed in righteousness divine'. Give Wesley's balance between Jesus being 'My living head'—Lord of his life— and 'No condemnation now I dread'—the Freedom of the Road, and the certainty of heaven: 'Bold I approach the eternal throne', an echo of Paul in 2 Timothy 4:8.

As a conclusion, take the very first two lines: make them a question for everyone. Who will come on Freedom Road? Trust Jesus!

5.3 *Amazing Grace*

Bible reading: Romans 3:19–26. Also Isaiah 6:3; 2 Corinthians 4:6.

Audience: Any occasion when 'Amazing Grace' is sung; songs of praise services; brass band concerts (if they will play it after you have spoken).

Aim: To show how amazing God's grace is, and to help people receive this undeserved love through Jesus.

Handy hint: A one-minute talk is in GRACE = God's riches at Christ's expense.

Visual aid: A series of acetates which builds the acrostic would work well: you could have the letters GRACE on all the time, adding to them for each point.

Outline: A jokey opening about the meanings of 'grace' you will not be taking (his Grace the Archbishop; what you say before eating; the girl next door) will set the scene for 'Amazing Grace'. They will love the word 'acrostic'— explain that it means taking the letters of GRACE: can they guess each one? That should hold their attention: especially with two words for each!

G = glory of God. Quote Romans 3:23–24. God is great

(Isaiah 6:3)! John Stott says: 'You cannot fix God at the end of a telescope or a microscope and say, "How interesting": God is not "interesting". He is profoundly unsettling' (from *Basic Christianity*). Talk about this.

R = requirement of right: 'His justice' (v.25). 'We uphold the law' (v.31). God expects perfection, hence verse 20 'It is the straight-edge of the Law that shows how crooked we are' (Phillips).

A = agony of all. Alan Dale's paraphrase of verse 23 is, 'We have all done wrong; none of us has lived as splendidly as God intended him to live.' Sir Francis Chichester (round-the-world yachtsman) said: 'Life is all a failure in the end.' Speak of where you know you have failed, sharing the agony.

C = compassion of Christ. He brought the glory (2 Corinthians 4:6), kept the right, and suffered the agony. GRACE = God's riches at Christ's expense. Draw out the wonder of verse 24. Verses 21 and 22 mean no trying by us to do it, so:

E = exclusion of effort.

Will we react as verse 26 asks? We will then be able to say, with John Newton:

> Amazing Grace, how sweet the sound,
> That saved a wretch like me.

5.4 The Two Faces of Christmas

Bible reading: John 1:1–14. Also 2 Corinthians 5:19.

Audience: Anyone at Christmas.

Aim: To invite people to be reconciled to God.

Illustration: You must have 'Hark the herald angels sing' somewhere in the service. 'It came upon the midnight clear' is fairly necessary, too, and must include the verse which begins, 'Yet with the woes of sin and strife. . .'

Outline: Enthuse about great Christmas carols. 'Hark the herald' is ranked among the four greatest hymns in the English language. Say how it contains a big 'today' word: 'reconciled'. Give one or two examples of (anonymous) people you know who need it: parent/child, wife/husband, manager/sports person. Explain how we all need the word when it comes to us and God, separated by sin.

Three cheers for Christmas! Show how the Bethlehem stable produced the Saviour: by his death he would remove sin, reconciling us to God (2 Corinthians 5:19). What are we waiting for? Why isn't the world like that? 'It came upon . . .' has a very sad verse, which talks about the woes of sin and strife causing 2,000 years of wrong, and man, at war with man, not hearing the 'herald angels sing'.

Talk briefly about your busy life, and how you need to 'hush your noise' to 'hear the angels sing'. The gospel for Christmas Day, John 1:1–14, speaks of the two faces of Christmas in verses 11 and 12. The tragedy is verse 11— often repeated today. The triumph of verse 12 can be ours.

Who will be reconciled to God today? Which face of Christmas looks at you?

6. Ladies First

This is the first of six sections for specific groupings, where a talk can be especially tailored for those present. A number of talks in each section can be extended or amended to include others.

6.1 Be a Martyr?

Bible references: Psalm 84:10; Matthew 21:17; Luke 10:38–42; John 11:5, 20–27; 12:1–3; Romans 10:9.

Audience: Ladies, especially older ladies.

Aim: To explain the good and the hard parts of being a real Christian.

Handy hint: Research Martha in a good commentary, so she will live in your talk.

Outline: A small pun to start: Christianity may not mean being a martyr, but it often is being a Martha. Give a quick background sketch of her: Bethany home, sister of Mary and Lazarus, home as a base for Jesus near Jerusalem. What made her a follower of Jesus? Two things:

First, she *believed* in Jesus. Give a brief background to the meeting of Martha and Jesus in John 11:20–27. She takes her problems, burdens and grief to him: do we? Show the greatness of Jesus' question in verses 25 and 26, and her excellent reply (v.27), fulfilling the definition of a Christian in Romans 10:9. Talk about Jesus as Saviour through the cross, bringing life through the resurrection. Barclay: 'Christianity does not mean arguing about Jesus: it means meeting Jesus.' He *is* the 'Son of God'. Ask who is trusting him, and who will do so today.

Secondly, she *belonged* to Jesus. This meant *sharing his word*. Say how glad you are with the honesty of the Bible, as we see the good and bad of its heroes and heroines. Martha had to learn a big lesson: walk through the embarrassing (for Martha) incident in Luke 10:38–42. We need to make time for Jesus: say how hard this is in your busy life, and how you succeed—and fail.

It also meant *sharing his work*. You could read John 12:1–3. Mary is the heroine, with her gift; Lazarus the hero, back from the dead. And Martha? She gets two words: ironic ones, 'Martha' is Aramaic for 'lady', who should have been served. Maybe she got leftovers (you might compare with being 'a doorkeeper': Psalm 84:10). She opened her home for Jesus (Matthew 21:17). She worked for Jesus because she loved him. The visitor to a leprosy colony saw a missionary washing a leper's feet: 'I wouldn't do that for a thousand dollars.' 'No,' she replied, 'neither would I.'

A great ending is to quote John 11:5, and show whose name is first. Jesus loves us too: will we not believe in him, and belong to him?

6.2 What's It Like to Know Jesus?

Bible references: Luke 1:26–38; John 14:6; John 11:17–44; Mark 15:40–41; Matthew 28:1–10; John 4:4–30; Luke 10:38–42; John 12:1–8; Mark 1:29–31.

Audience: Women of all ages.

Aim: By taking as examples different women who met Jesus, to show what it means for a woman to become and be a Christian.

Handy hint: Use illustrations from your own life, and contemporary Christian women—famous, or known to you personally. This will give back-up to the Bible characters. People stories always go well.

Outline: Apologise for the poor 'image' some Christians present for their faith. But Jesus still has a great attraction—what is it like to know him?

It means *truth*. Christians have not been conned: Mary, Jesus' mother knew the virgin birth was true (never mind some bishops) and Martha found Jesus is 'the Resurrection and the Life'. The truth leads to *triumph*, as the women see Jesus beat sin as he dies on the cross, and meet him on resurrection morning. Show how this triumph has touched your life, and the wonderful difference it makes.

Be honest: knowing Jesus is demanding. The woman who met him by the well had to spend *time* talking, and telling her neighbours. Martha was chided for her lack of time. For some it means *treasure*—as the woman with the ointment found; and for those who watched Jesus going to die it meant *tears*. This is a different way of life.

Most of all, knowing Jesus means *trust*. Peter's mother-in-law is a good example—and you will want to use your own story, too. Finally, invite your hearers to make a simple response by trusting the one who is true, for the great but demanding life he gives.

6.3 Look What I've Found!

Bible passage: John 20:11–18. Also John 19:25.

Audience: Women; Easter congregations.

Aim: To bring the great news of Easter to women, using the first person who met Jesus alive from the dead as the heroine.

Handy hint: Capture the excitement!

Outline: The Koreans say: 'Expect the unexpected, and in the unexpected, expect Christ.' It was never more true than for one woman, one morning—the morning that changed the world. Some sort of dramatic opening like this will set the scene for the brilliant resurrection account seen through the eyes of Mary Magdalene.

Thumb-nail sketch her background: not good, not special, not important—yet she really loved Jesus, and followed faithfully. With other women she had seen Jesus die (John 19:25). Now she is devastated, as she comes to the tomb to embalm the body.

Mary *looks*. You could compare how she nearly looked for the right thing with the way we do the same. She was looking for a tomb and a corpse. What do we look for in our own faith—a church, ceremony, services? Mary

should have looked for Jesus—and so should we. Talk
about how easily recognisable he is: the nailprints, the
risen glory. Mary wasn't ready: but Jesus was!

So Mary *finds*. But who found whom? Moffat translates
the word in verse 11 as 'sobbing'. Share how you are
moved by Jesus, and that a 'stiff upper lip' may hold
back real and good emotion. Jesus had got up before
Mary! It is time to meet the risen Jesus, as he speaks
our name. Talk about your own personal encounter with
Jesus, and how you know him one-to-one.

Finally Mary *shares*. The 'go and tell' of verse 17 is
obeyed in verse 18. Good news is too precious to keep
locked up.

You could wrap up the talk with, 'The best day of my
life,' said Mary. We can have that, too, as we meet the
risen Jesus.

6.4 Your Call!

Bible passage: John 11:17–44.

Audience: Primarily women; good for evangelistic services.

Aim: To show that the call of Jesus is for each one of us.

Outline: Speak of a moment in your life when a big invitation/summons came (to go to meet royalty, to have a vital interview, to report to the head teacher, to lunch with the boss). How would it be if the King of kings called; if you heard: 'The Master has come, and calls for you'? You could use the current equivalent of the old phone advert, 'It's for you!' or the lottery's 'It could be you!'

Explain the background to John 11:28: the three in the family, Lazarus dying, Jesus arriving and meeting Martha, leading to the verse. Now talk about who 'The Master (Teacher)' is, and how he has come (heaven to Bethlehem, to the cross, to the empty tomb, to now). He is the Master over life and death, sin and hell. With Mary, Jesus was the answer to all her hurts—even her frustration and implied anger of verse 32.

Jesus called for Mary. Talk about how you sensed his

call on your life. Explain how Christianity is both shared and personal, and how Jesus always comes to us individually. Speak about the greatness of the call, and the love with which it is made.

This should lead naturally to Mary's response in verse 31: 'How quickly she got up and went.' Perhaps you were hesitant or shy yourself: that would be good to share. No doubt Jesus would have raised Lazarus whether Mary had come or not: but she might have missed the blessing.

Come back to the key verse. Eyeball your audience: 'It's for you!' Help them get up quickly and meet Jesus.

6.5 Just a Woman?

Bible passage: John 4:4–42 (the reading could end at verse 26).

Audience: Women.

Aim: To show how important women are to God, and that any woman can trust Jesus Christ.

Handy hint: If you are a man giving this talk, they will turn off completely at the slightest suggestion that you are being patronising!

Outline: 'Sometimes it's hard to be a woman,' says the song. 'Twas ever thus. If there is still a struggle for rights today, say how impossible things were 2,000 years ago. Speak also of the disadvantage of following God and not being a Jew: thus a foreign woman had two major problems.

Set the scene: the lonely well, the heat at midday, the disciples in the town, and the woman who comes for water and meets the Son of God: quite an encounter! Ask how any of us would feel, meeting Jesus—express your own reservations (not good/important/special enough). What a shock the story is, even 2,000 years and much liberation later.

Make something of the splendidly ordinary greeting—
'Can I have a drink?' (v.7). Jesus is normal—and treats us
that way, too! Try to get across the three offers Jesus
makes to this unnamed woman, and that these are for
your audience today. Make the incident live, as you bring
out that he offers:

1. A new today. 'Living water' (v.10). Show the new
life he gives now, and the difference this makes for you.

2. A new yesterday. Explain the 'five husbands' in
verses 16–18, and how the woman calls Jesus, 'A man
who told me everything I ever did' (v.29). With her
village, she discovered he 'really is the Saviour of the
world' (v.42). Talk about Jesus as Saviour, dealing with
all our yesterdays, able to forgive and make new through
the cross.

3. A new tomorrow. 'A spring of water welling up to
eternal life' (v.14). By his Holy Spirit we are made new
for ever.

As a conclusion, invite your audience to meet Jesus at
their 'well' today, as he comes to make past, present and
future new.

6.6 Reach Out

Bible passage: Luke 8:40–48. Also Isaiah 53:5; Matthew 9:18–26; Mark 5:21–34; Acts 4:12.

Audience: Ladies; older people; guest services.

Aim: To show how ordinary people can trust Jesus.

Handy hint: The passage is paralleled in Matthew 9:18–26 and Mark 5:21–34. Both are worth checking for further ideas (especially Mark). This is a very moving, personal story. Capture the beauty of it.

Outline: Why aren't all Bibles red, with 'This is your life' on them? You could say you often feel it is telling your story—and that is how it is here. Or: some people never seem important: here is a lady who only gets in because she interrupts an important person's story. Either way, get to the unnamed woman of Luke 8:43.

Make the story live. Explain the problem of her illness making her 'unclean', and having to keep away from worship, as our sins keep us from God. She did her best, spending everything to buy cures. Speak of your doing your best, but never being perfect. Others may not have known: do others think we are wonderful, when we know the truth?

Here comes her answer: someone who can help. He is the one Peter speaks of in Acts 4:12. He's died for us, and lives to set things right. Go on to Peter's half joke in verse 45. Everyone rubbed shoulders with Jesus—but only she came with faith to be healed. You could share your sorrow that many hear of Jesus, but few respond. Enjoy the 'immediately' of verse 44: she is 'healed' (v.48), echoes of Isaiah 53:5, as Jesus takes our sins away.

The woman has to let the world know, as Jesus calls her out (v.45). Like her, we are afraid, maybe only touching his cloak (v.44): but it is enough. The Roman Catholic Mass, and Anglo-Catholic Eucharist, each has the lovely prayer: 'Lord, I am not worthy to receive you, but only say the word and I shall be healed.'

Invite a brave reaching out to Jesus, as you close.

6.7 Washing Day

Bible passage: John 13:1–15. Also John 12:3; 1 John 1:7–8.

Audience: Women, especially ones with children; older women (and men).

Aim: To take a very ordinary, everyday subject to explain what Jesus does for us, and expects from us.

Handy hint: Be simple, with stories from your own experience, especially at the start of the talk.

Visual aid: An old mangle, or wash-board, would make an excellent introduction. A scrubbing brush would do.

Outline: A little nostalgia will work wonders to start: your mother or—even better—granny, with the great Monday washing day (don't forget the visual aid): the hard work, even compared with today. Recall the steamed-up windows, the pulley on the ceiling for drying, the smells. If you have no memories, talk to an older woman and borrow hers!

Being a Christian is like washing day: Jesus had a special one—not on Monday, but Thursday evening. Describe, so they feel they are there, the events of John

13:1–9. Get to 1 John 1:8, and then back to 1 John 1:7. We need a 'washing day'—and a daily clean up, like Peter. Are you clean? Don't rush this part of the talk: speak of Jesus cleansing you.

Part 2 is what that will mean as your life is changed. It means serving Jesus: refer back to John 12:3, and Mary giving her best for her 'washing day' of Jesus' feet. F.B. Meyer, at eighty-two said: 'All I want is to be one of God's errand boys.' It will also mean a 'washing day' for others: give a couple of concrete suggestions as to what John 13:12–15 means today. Hence C.H. Spurgeon's words: 'If you want to give a tract to a hungry man, wrap it up in a sandwich.'

Maybe it is not Monday: but today is washing day!

7. Mainly Men

As Section 6 is for women, so this set is a 'men only' group, though some will work for others, too.

7.1 Look Out—It's God!

Bible passage: Luke 19:1–10. Also Matthew 7:7; Luke 15:20.

Audience: Men; church congregations.

Aim: To help people meet Jesus in a one-to-one encounter, using the Jesus-Zacchaeus meeting.

Handy hint: This is a simple, direct incident: aim for your talk to be the same. Make this old, true story come to life again.

Outline: Start by saying how you would like to explain what it is like for someone (a man, if 'men only') to meet Jesus: so here is an incident they may have heard before, about one man who did meet Jesus: read to them Luke 19:1–10. Say how we all love Zacchaeus, because we are so like him. Give a quick thumb-nail sketch of the little (v.3) tax-man (v.1), who got it wrong sometimes (v.7), and knew it (v.8). Somehow he realised Jesus liked his sort of people, and he went looking: do we?

Ask what Zacchaeus saw when Jesus came. You are trying to show Jesus was true man and true God. Jesus was a man, like Zacchaeus, and us. Talk of the human side: his tiredness, sorrow, joy, fun, friendships—and death: the examples of these you enjoy most are best. But Zacchaeus also saw God: explain how Jesus is God's Son—the most wonderful person Zacchaeus, and we, could ever meet. He wanted to meet someone special—he met the best (as promised in Matthew 7:7).

But—a big but—be sure to show how Jesus was already coming down the road to meet Zacchaeus, even coming over to his tree (v.5). There are echoes of the prodigal son's father in Luke 15:20. Say how Jesus has been looking for us, his road coming via Bethlehem, the cross, the empty tomb, right to now. Make your audience feel that Jesus is here to meet each one personally. Speak of his love for each of them, even to his death. As Jesus knew Zacchaeus by name (v.5), he knows us.

The call of verse 5 is for us: show the need to respond, and that Zacchaeus could have stayed in his tree. You will want to show the way everyone saw (v.7), and the changes (v.8), which look hard. But he came 'gladly' (v.6), and Jesus gave 'salvation' (v.9), and verse 10 is for us.

As you have made the talk personal, call for a personal response, re-emphasising the words of Jesus in verse 5. You may want to include, 'I did that,' so it is an 'us', not a 'you'.

7.2 It's Hard (Being Hard)

Bible passage: Psalm 81. Also Deuteronomy 32:3–4; Psalm 61:2; Ezekiel 36:26; Matthew 4:4; 7:24; 13:5–6, 20–21; Luke 23:53; 1 Peter 2:4–6.

Audience: Men.

Aim: To overcome men's opposition to the gospel, and to help them find the one who will bless their lives.

Handy hint: Don't be afraid of talking 'straight': sometimes a throat-grabbing approach works best. You need the nerve!

Outline: They say that men are tough nuts to crack: open by telling them that! As Paul Simon wrote in the early 1960s: 'I've built walls, a fortress deep and mighty that none may penetrate: I am a rock.'

What makes us men so hard when it comes to God? What do we gain from it? Are we right? (Make it 'us', not 'you'; identify with them.) Is it our pride? Or fear? Recall Jesus talking of stony ground, caused by persecution (Matthew 13:5–6, 20–21): we are afraid of being different, or of failing. We are hardened by our wrong (Ezekiel 36:26).

Good news! There is someone even harder: God is *the*

Rock (Deuteronomy 32:3–4). Jesus came, the hard man who refused to turn rocks to bread for selfish ends (Matthew 4:4), allowed his life to be broken for us on the cross, and was buried in a rock-tomb (Luke 23:53). He is alive, and we can build on him as the Rock (1 Peter 2:4–6), and be wise as we follow his way (Matthew 7:24). Say how you, as a hard man, are not ashamed to come to Christ, because he is the best and hardest of all: as David said, 'Lead me to the rock that is higher than I' (Psalm 61:2). Invite your audience to do that themselves.

What if they do? Get to Psalm 81, and its superb ending: 'With honey from the rock I would satisfy you.' God, through Jesus, offers release from sin (vv.6–7), a new life (v.10), as long as we let God be our God (v.9). Who wants verse 12? Not me!

Who will come to the Rock, for life?

7.3 Count Me In

Bible reading: Hebrews 11:32–12:2.

Audience: Men only.

Aim: To show men that, whatever they are like now, they can be men of God.

Handy hint: The Outline sketches half a dozen Bible characters. Familiarise yourself with their histories. Some background reading on each of them would help you to make them live.

Outline: Open with how brilliant men are! We could fix the national football/cricket/rugby team, run the country, feed the world: we are great men. So what stops us being men of God? Because we look at the heroes of faith, and could never match them.

Explain how Hebrews 11 is full of these men, and you want to prove from them that we can all be men of God. Here are a few: verse 32. What were they like?

Gideon—full of doubt ('Who me?' Recall the 'fleece' incidents). But he gave God his doubts: men of God do doubt sometimes, but still go with God.

Barak—the coward, who would not go to battle without a woman alongside him. But he did go. Explain how we men are afraid to be God's men: we need to give him our fear.

Samson and Jephthah—the bad guys! We do sin, and feel unworthy to be God's men. They made it because 'the Spirit of the Lord' came on them: that is how you do it, when Jesus forgives you.

David—the nobody: not even lined up with his brothers by his own father to meet Samuel. We feel insignificant: but God calls people like that.

If you want, you can tackle Samuel and a couple of prophets: but you should by now have shown that the most unlikely can be God's men—you, your hearers. If we dare, and do, show the two-fold result. First, victory (vv.33–35, first half). Jesus will give us victories over sin, and a Holy Spirit filled life. Second, total cost (vv.35–38): don't pretend there is no cost.

Why should we be God's men? One reason: 12:1–2: because Jesus was God's man for us. Speak of his total commitment, and then call for that response to him.

7.4 Is God on Your Side?

Bible reading: Psalm 124. Also Genesis 3:4; John 8:34, 36, 44; Ephesians 6:12; 1 Peter 5:8.

Audience: Men; churchgoers.

Aim: To help people realise how much they need Christ, and his willingness to be on their side.

Handy hint: Psalm 124 is a series of great word-pictures: some graphic verbal painting is needed.

Outline: Have you heard a big Welsh choir sing 'Who is on the Lord's side?' (tune, Rachie)? If not, say how preachers often ask, 'Who is on God's side?' You want to turn it round and ask your hearers, 'Do you think God is on your side?'

Because if not . . . . This is a good place to read Psalm 124 (it is not long). Enthuse about David's skill as a word-painter, and his three images of the force of evil:

Its *power*, swallowing us alive, like a lion (v.3). Coventry Cathedral has a great mural of Michael and the devil, the enemy of our souls (1 Peter 5:8, John 8:44) who attacks us, and always has (Genesis 3:4). The opposition is too strong (Ephesians 6:12).

Its *speed* (v.5). Shepherd David pictures the steep-sided

118

Judean wadi beds: sheep there when the rain comes are washed away, with no escape from the flash floods. Similarly, evil gets us (v.4).

Its *cunning*, as we get trapped like a bird by a clever fowler (v.7). We become slaves to sin (John 8:34).

As you paint these pictures, don't give the answer too soon. Now you can re-read verses 6 and 7. Where is there help? Verse 8 tells us of 'the Lord'. Explain how Jesus is Lord, the lion-slayer, defeating the devil on the cross, rising again to pull us from the flood, cutting open the net (John 8:36). Tell them how he has done this for you.

Invite your hearers to call Jesus over to them, to be on their side, to give them the joy David, and you, have found.

7.5 Just Right!

Bible passage: John 5:1–15. Also 2 Corinthians 6:2.

Audience: Men; churchgoers, sceptics.

Aims: To show that each person is just right to become a Christian and, conversely, Christ is just right for each of us.

Handy hint: Don't be worried about reading the passage in a non-Christian setting. Explain that you have a man you want to talk about, that he has a great story, and you are going to read it before you share it. Then do it! Our fear of what people will think if we read a longish Bible passage is in ourselves. Our audience is waiting to hear.

Outline: Why not start with a provocative hot potato, eg 'Isn't it time you became a Christian?' or 'Today's the day—it's for you!' or 'Who dares, wins'? Or ease into it with, 'Perhaps it has never felt right up till now for you to consider being a Christian. Let me try and change your mind today.'

Or simply paint the picture of Jesus meeting the man: the pool, the crowds of sick people, the boredom, the hopelessness. Grab the start of verse 5 'One who was there': one among many—that is how God sees us, as we are. Here comes Jesus: thumb-nail sketch him—his love, his concern, his authority and power. He sums up the situation with his question in verse 6.

A crazy question—with only one answer: but the man hedges. Describe the forgiveness and new life Jesus offers today, and a few of our excuses. If you made excuses before letting Christ help, men will appreciate your honesty and identify with you: especially if you still keep him at arm's length in certain circumstances. Show the double remedy Jesus gives in verse 14.

Explain the problem in verses 9 and 10, and how we say, 'Yes—but not today.' You could refer to 2 Corinthians 6:2 here. It was—and is—the right day.

The right man—the right help—the right day: wrap it up with: 'Do it now.'

8. Golden Oldies

A quarter of the population is over sixty, and the percentage is rising. The following outlines seek to address the needs of the older generation, and their situations.

8.1 New for Old

Bible references: Numbers 21:4–9; John 3:1–16.

Audience: Older people.

Aim: To show that, however old we are, God can make us new.

Handy hint: If you are old, you are onto a winner. Identify with your audience with stories from your own life, and how you felt about the old when you were young, and what it now feels like. Show the difference Jesus makes in your older life. If you are younger than your audience, beware of patronising. Speak with love and concern.

Outline: Talk about growing old, including the definition of old age: 'Ten years older than you are!' Comment on what other people say about old people—patronising, pitying, ignoring, regarding as increasing problems. You could quote Lewis Carroll from *Alice in Wonderland*, 'You are old, Father William.' Didn't we think that about the old when we were young?

Admit that when you get older you also have no thought of much change. Aladdin's new-for-old lamps do not translate into new-for-old lives.

Which leads to the shock of discovering that God has other ideas. Describe the old Jewish leader, Nicodemus, visiting Jesus, and Jesus telling him he needed to be born all over again.

Re-create the visit verbally, especially 'Can a man be born when he is *old*?' Show how God's Spirit blows like the wind, and bring the audience to the climax of John 3:15–16. Use verse 15 as a story-teller, explaining what happened in Numbers 21, and how Jesus turned it to speak of himself. By so doing, we can have 'new for old'.

End with a call for us 'oldies' to let Jesus make us new.

8.2 Lighten Our Darkness

Bible references: Psalm 23; Isaiah 40:28; Malachi 3:6; Matthew 11:28; John 8:12; Philippians 1:21; Hebrews 13:5.

Audience: The elderly; the hurting; the bereaved.

Aim: To bring the light of God's love into the hurts of life.

Handy hint: Handle with care: be prepared for tears. Be gentle. While bringing in personal references, do not imagine it is possible to understand fully the pains of another: each suffering is, in some way, unique.

Outline: An anecdotal start would be good about the problems of the dark, eg 'I was walking home late the other evening when I fell down a pot-hole/tripped over a paving slab/kicked a cat . . . ' Life is often dark: how can we cope in the problems and pains we face as we get older?

Somewhere in the talk, it will help to quote two answers. These can be saved till the end, or introduced now and referred to when needed. The ancient 'Evening Prayer' says: 'Lighten our darkness we beseech Thee, O Lord, and by Thy great mercy defend us from all perils and dangers of this night. For the love of Thine only Son, our Saviour Jesus Christ.' Jesus said: 'I am the light of the world; he who follows me will not walk in darkness, but will have the light of life' (John 8:12).

Depending on the audience, all or some of the following 'darknesses' can be mentioned:

1. *The darkness of sin.* Getting older makes people aware of their failures: the might-have-beens, the if-onlys. The prayer speaks of 'our Saviour Jesus Christ'. We can offer his forgiveness to remove the darkness.

2. *Old age brings 'perils and dangers'.* Minds may wander. There are three signs of old age: grey hair, loss of memory, and . . . I can't remember the other one (!). The world changes ('Not like the old days'). Malachi 3:6 and Isaiah 40:28 help here.

3. *Loneliness.* Family move away, friends die. We live alone. Use Hebrews 13:5 and other verses to show that Jesus will 'never forsake'.

4. *Bereavement.* Probably the greatest darkness, especially of a partner, child or parent. Betsie ten Boom said to her sister Corrie, 'There is no pit so deep that he is not deeper': an echo of Psalm 23:4.

5. *Sickness.* Sight and hearing fail; it is hard to bounce back. Now is the time to do as Brother Lawrence said: 'Practise the presence of God.' We can respond to Jesus' invitation in Matthew 11:28.

6. *Dying.* The process is hard, but we can say with Paul, 'To die is gain' (Philippians 1:21).

Whichever you choose (there could be a series here!), revert to the Evening Prayer and John 8:12, and invite a quiet but real trust in the Saviour, who cares.

8.3 Restored

Bible references: Joel 1:1–4, 14, 19; 2:1, 11–13, 21–29; 3:14. Also Isaiah 44:22; Philippians 3:13–14; 1 John 1:7.

Audience: Older people; people whose lives have gone badly wrong (eg in prison).

Aim: To show how God not only forgives, but restores our lives to be as they always should have been.

Handy hint: The key verse is Joel 2:25. It is better for the title and theme to use an older Bible translation which says 'restore', rather than the NIV's 'repay'.

Outline: You can either start with those things that haunt us—memories, if-onlys, ghosts of days gone by—asking what we can do to erase the past; or say how impossible it is to change yesterday. But God can perform the most amazing miracle: you would like to prove it by explaining a great Bible promise: 'I will restore the years the locust has eaten' (Joel 2:25).

First, some background. If you have seen locusts, describe them. If not, remind people of what locusts do, eating everything green. The devastation is brilliantly detailed in Joel 1:1–4 (v.4 will do). As the land, so our lives. Few would agree with Edith Piaf, *'Non, je ne regrette rien'* (I regret nothing). How can wrong be righted, and our lives restored?

For our part, we must turn to God (Joel 1:14, 19), asking for his help. You will have to decide whether you, and your audience, can cope with Joel 2:1 and 2:11. However, Joel 2:12–13 is a very positive 'what if', and the lovely ending to 1 John 1:7 shows how God blesses us when we do repent. Have you an example you could share of when you turned to God for forgiveness?

On God's side, he makes a great Old Testament promise of his Holy Spirit in Joel 2:28–29, not leaving us empty when the wrong has been removed. Now for the great miracle in Joel 2:25. In 2:22 and 24 the size of the change is seen: gardens take ages to grow, but God makes it as if they had never been ruined (an echo of Isaiah 44:22).

As in 3:14, we have to decide. If we do, we can be as Paul in Philippians 3:13–14. Who will receive God's miracle?

8.4 Silver Threads

Bible references: Genesis 15:15; Psalms 37:25; 71:18; 92:14; Isaiah 46:4; John 14:27; Galatians 5:22–23.

Audience: The elderly.

Aim: To show that God saves his best for the oldies.

Outline: 'Darling, I am growing old, silver threads among the gold' (Ebenezer Rexford)—an old song! David said the same in Psalm 37:25. Ask if that equals being useless, forgotten, hopeless. Not to God! Tell your audience you have discovered something very exciting: God's best is for oldies. Three Ps for your talk:

God's *presence*. Isaiah 46:4 is a great offer: ask who has received it. Have we let God save us? Is he carrying us?

God's *purpose*. When we trust him, Psalm 92:14 shows how new life grows on old plants. Explain that life is no downward path for the Christian. You could mention the fruit of the Spirit in Galatians 5:22–23. If you are into poetry, it was Robert Browning, in his poem 'Rabbi ben Ezra', who said:

Grow old along with me,
The best is yet to be;

The last of life, for which the first was made.
Our times are in His hand.

Thirdly, God's *peace*. God made a lovely promise to Abraham in Genesis 15:15, that he would die in peace. We need peace now, and at the last. Show how Jesus promised peace just before his own death (John 14:27). Do we know that?

To enable your audience to respond, there is a brilliant prayer in Psalm 71:18: 'Even when I am old and grey, do not forsake me, O God.' Invite such a heartfelt, simple response.

8.5 Up You Go

Bible passage: John 12:27–36. Also Mark 8:34.

Audience: Older people.

Aim: To show how Jesus wants to draw us up to himself.

Handy hint: Tailor the talk to the age group. If older, a reference to 'The Old Rugged Cross' would go well (till recently it was Britain's Number 1 favourite hymn). If younger, the talk itself can be more 'rugged'.

Outline: In St Mark's Church, Harrogate, North Yorkshire, is a great stained-glass east window, showing Christ on the cross. Under the cross are the words: 'And I, if I be lifted up from the earth, will draw all men unto me' (from the Authorised Version of John 12:32). Recall a stained-glass window you know of the crucifixion, and fit that verse to it, as a verbally visual introduction.

Why does Jesus want to lift us up to his cross? Because there he can rescue us from sin (v.31: you could bring in 'The Old Rugged Cross' here). He saves us from the power of the evil one. By so doing, we are forgiven. David Bubbers gives a lovely comment: 'Mercy is God not giving us what we do deserve; Grace is God giving us what we do not deserve.' Speak of how special all this is to you.

You may want to add something of our lives being healed at the cross, quoting Edward Shillito:

> The other gods were strong, but thou wast weak.
> They rode, but thou didst stumble to a throne.
> But to our wounds only God's wounds can speak,
> And not a god has wounds, but thou alone.

Don't miss Mark 8:34: being drawn to the cross means sharing the cost.

Secondly, Jesus draws us up to his glory. He is alive, and we enter his new life, and light (v.36). Speak of the wonder of this, and of heaven (the latter especially for the old). You could recall the absent-minded G.K. Chesterton's telegram to his wife: 'Am in Market Harborough. Where should I be?' Her single-word reply read, 'Home.' Ask if we are going 'home' to Jesus.

The beginning of verse 36 gives a good way to end: you could quote verse 32 again, as you ask for a quiet response of trust.

9. Youth's 'Yes'

Young people especially respond to a challenge. These outlines may have some strong meat in them, so they can be used for those of all ages who will dare to do great things for God. But they will prove most effective with teens and twenties.

9.1 How Much Is It?

Bible references: Isaiah 52:13–53:10; 55:1; Matthew 27:46; Luke 9:25, 58; 12:20; 14:25–35; 18:22, 29–30; Romans 3:23.

Audience: Young people; men; church congregations.

Aim: To show the balance between being a Christian and a non-Christian, and that there is a price to be paid either way.

Handy hint: You could start with the cost to us, bringing in what Christ paid second, leading naturally to the tragic cost of rejection by us.

Outline: Moan about the cost of living (which could be the title for the talk!): something will have gone up in price (petrol, baked beans, beer). What a lot life costs.

Get right into how much your life really costs—to Jesus Christ. You could divide his death on the cross into three costs, with Isaiah 52 and 53 as the basis. Explain how we are away from God because of his perfection, and our sin (Romans 3:23). Jesus came to take the results of that in our place. It cost him everything *physically* (Isaiah 52:13–4): talk about the beatings, the nails, the pain and agony. He suffered *mentally* (53:3–4): refer to the degradation of being spat on, and the loneliness when the disciples ran away. Most of all, it cost him *spiritually* (53:10), as he was separated from his Father (Matthew 27:46). Why all this cost? Explain the significance of Isaiah 53:4–5: he paid for us.

Now to the nitty-gritty: there is a cost for us, too. Invite your audience to sit down and face it using the two stories in Luke 14:25–35, including those serious warnings in verses 26 and 27. You could also refer to the rich young ruler (Luke 18:22), and Jesus' comment about himself in Luke 9:58. So it does not seem all doom and gloom, Luke 18:29–30 is a nicely balanced text. Don't play down this cost. For some to whom you speak it may mean life and death: it will certainly take all they've got. Do you have an example of someone you know who died for their faith (a very recent one is better than many years ago)?

But there is another cost—for those who turn from Christ's offer to pay for them. Luke 9:25 is a strong, true question: one we hear infrequently. Luke 12:20 is powerful, too. Speak of what people miss when they miss Jesus: his forgiveness, love, life and—ultimately— heaven itself. Speak of the joy of giving everything to Jesus, because he gives everything to us. In a strong talk, be sure to end on a strong positive, as you throw out the challenge: who dares, wins!

9.2 Everything You've Got

Bible references: Matthew 9:9–13; Mark 2:13–17; Luke 5:27–31.

Audience: Young people; men.

Aim: Through a study of the call of Matthew, to show what it means to be a disciple of Jesus.

Handy hint: Check all three readings to get every facet of the call.

Outline: Set the scene: a wandering preacher; a man with a cosy and lucrative job; the simplicity of the meeting and the directness of the call (Matthew 9:9). Aim to show the finality and totality of this for Matthew—and for us today. A reference to each of the three passages will give three features:

1. *His job*: he left it (Matthew 9:9). That would mean money, too. Not everyone who follows Jesus leaves their work, but Jesus becomes Lord over our working life, and money. Show how Christianity is not 'Sundays only'. Would we leave our job if Jesus told us to?

2. *His friends* (Mark 2:15–16): everyone got to know. His

private, social and home life were affected. You could share one or two embarrassing moments where areas of your life became invaded by Jesus.

3. *His total life* (Luke 5:28): he 'left everything'. Have you a modern example of someone (famous/known to you) who has done this?

What a challenge! Everything given to Jesus. Say that you have put them off enough—now for the good news: three again.

1. He spent three years walking the lanes of Israel with God's Son. Ask who people would most like to spend the rest of their lives with: maybe they *will*! They can also have Jesus—the very best, with his life, power, friendship: talk about how special this is for you.

2. The world-changing events of the cross, resurrection and Pentecost involved Matthew: Jesus died, rose, sent his Spirit, for him—and us. Share these as vital for your life.

3. Jokingly ask if anyone has studied Matthew's tax returns! He could have written all his life for nothing: but his Gospel, which God got him to write, gives the first twenty-eight chapters of the New Testament. What will we do which will last for ever? God has eternal plans: who will come and know them?

Admit it is a big decision—as for Matthew. Who will hear Jesus, and 'follow him'?

9.3 Time-to-go Time

Bible references: Joshua 1:9; John 6:66–69; 14:6.

Audience: Primarily church-going young people—eleven to twenty-five. Appropriate for other churchgoers too.

Aim: To challenge the audience to become seriously committed to Jesus Christ. It is unusual because we normally use the angle 'Please stay'. This different approach of 'Are you going?' may strike a deep chord.

Handy hint: This is a go-for-it message, with some strong meat and straight talking. Be sure to lighten the pressure occasionally with jokes and asides—can you do a Churchillian voice for his quote?

Outline: Recall your excitement at growing up, moving out and on: college, university, first flat, new girl/boy friend—just a couple of good, fun examples. We grow away from our childhood: will you grow away from your young faith at the same time?

Many grow tired of the hardships of Christianity. The bloke in bed, yelled at by his mother on Sunday to go to church, asked for three good reasons why he should: 'First, I'm your mother and I'm telling you to go. Second, you're forty-one, and old enough to go by yourself. Third—you're the vicar!' Tell it well!

Get into John 6:66, to show people have left since the beginning. Jesus even gave his closest disciples the option. Speak honestly about how hard it is to stay when most people are not Christians. Give an example or two from your own life of the cost of following Christ. The easy life may be away from God.

Come to Peter's response in John 6:68–69. Was Peter right? Show how events proved him so—the cross, resurrection, the coming of the Holy Spirit. To leave Jesus is to go from the truth. However strong the opposition, hang in with Jesus. Winston Churchill (do the voice): 'Never give in; never give in; never, never, never, never. Never yield to force. Never yield to the apparently overwhelming might of the enemy.'

Close with Joshua 1:9, having set it in the context of young Joshua urged forward by old Moses. Call for full commitment.

9.4 OK—I'll Go!

Bible passage: Isaiah 6. Also Exodus 3:5; Psalm 51:5; Isaiah 64:6; Matthew 28:19; Luke 5:8; John 3:16; Romans 3:10; 5:8; 1 Timothy 1:15.

Audience: Young people; Christians needing to be challenged regarding outreach.

Aim: To show that we can be Christians, and take the good news, if we really know God.

Handy hint: Check a good Bible commentary for the political and religious background to Isaiah 6, to show the vital significance of this encounter.

Outline: The American phrase 'eyeball to eyeball' is a possible way of asking how would people feel at meeting God in a close encounter. Explain that 2,500 years ago one man did that, and how we can today.

A brief background may be good, but make it short, dramatic and interesting: the king of forty years dead, the rampaging Assyrians, the sinful nation, and Isaiah in the Temple. He sees the greatness of God: you could pick up the features of verse 1 (size), verses 2 and 3 (holiness), verse 4 (power) to show that God is bigger than all the problems—then and now—the Almighty.

Isaiah's reaction (v.5) is typical of all who got this close, eg Moses (Exodus 3:5), Peter (Luke 5:8), Paul (1 Timothy 1:15). No wonder he later spoke of sin in the words of Isaiah 64:6, echoed in Romans 3:10, and by David in Psalm 51:5. Humanists see no sin, because they do not stand in the powerful searchlight of God, so see no shadow. Speak of your awareness of your life's shortcomings.

Enthuse about verses 6 and 7, bringing in verses like John 3:16 and Romans 5:8. Ask your audience if they have let God burn away their sin. Only then can God make the call in verse 8: and Isaiah can reply as he does out of gratitude.

If there is time, a comment could be made on the rarely read rest of the chapter, where Isaiah is not promised success, though the end of the chapter's implied promise of Jesus gives ultimate hope. God looks for faithfulness, not success, as we follow the command of Jesus in Matthew 28:19.

Your ending is fairly obvious: back to verse 8 for the call, and response. Who will say it now?

9.5 Multiplication by Division

Bible passages: John 6:53–54; 7:37–52.

Audience: Young people; would work with men, too.

Aim: To challenge to a brave, clear-cut commitment to Christ.

Handy hint: This is a strong talk; lighten it occasionally with a fun comment.

Outline: The key verse is John 7:43: 'The people were divided because of Jesus.' You might begin with your problem being that of all speakers—we like to be liked! But Christianity has always multiplied by division, ie there is a make-your-mind-up time to enable new followers of Jesus to say 'Yes', which means some can say 'No'.

That is how it has always been—you could bring in the key verse here. What divided them then? It was their response to what Jesus was offering. He offered blood (John 6:53–54). Explain how offensive this sounds, and why it is vital for our salvation. He offered water (John 8:37–39). It sounded weak: show how vital it is for us to be filled with the Holy Spirit.

How did they react? The same as today. Those *against*

(all in John 7) included *doubters* (v.41). How could they trust this man from Galilee? Rabbi Lionel Blue jokes of the man who fell over a cliff and got caught on a tree. 'Is there anyone up there?' he shouted. A voice answered, 'Trust me, and let go. I will catch you.' To which the man replied, 'Is there anyone else up there?'

Some *hated* Jesus (v.44). Speak of how many in our country want to have nothing to do with him. A concrete, recent example here for each sort of opposition will earth what you are saying. Others *mocked* (vv.48–49). Today, people belittle Christians, especially those 'born again'. Similarly, the *scoffers* (v.52) did not need Jesus. 'I'm good enough' is an echo of Coué, the French philosopher: 'Every day in every way I'm becoming better and better.' (In the end he committed suicide!)

Was anyone *for* Jesus? Only one is named: Nicodemus (v.50). Who dares be the one for Jesus, accepting the blood of forgiveness and the water of his Holy Spirit?

Ask for volunteers!

10. Don't Forget the Children!

Many people look back to childhood as the time when they made their first steps of faith. Children need to be helped in a very sensitive, unpressured way. They can then discover a real relationship with the Lord Jesus.

10.1 Four Men, Four Trees

Bible references: (in the order of the Outline) Genesis 3:8–9; John 1:47–48; Luke 19:4–5; John 19:17–18. If you need a reading, make it Luke 19:1–10. Or get four people to read the four sets of two verses each.

Audience: Children; family services; adults via the youngsters.

Aim: To show that Jesus is the answer to our past, present and future.

Visuals: A tree for each reading (big pictures/acetates): someone peeping from behind the first, sitting under the second, up the third. And a simple, empty, wooden cross for the last.

Handy hints: Lots of audience participation—questions throughout, eg Who's this? Why's he there? What's he doing? Be prepared for weird and wonderful answers (eg 'Jonah' for the second one!). Tell each story to half way, then bring in the fourth tree, and show how Jesus fits all the others.

Outline: Show *Tree 1*. Who is it? Adam. Explain how sad it is for him and Eve to be hiding from a loving God.

Children do understand wrong—sin—don't belittle it. We all need an answer, like Adam, for the wrong in our past. Where?

Tree 2. Will anyone guess Nathaniel? Give a few clues. He and friend Philip want someone to follow in the future.

Tree 3. Our old favourite Zacchaeus. So like us, needing help today with his life. Can he spot someone who'll give it?

No need to guess *Tree 4*. The person was broken like the tree. Go back to the first tree: he died for them—and us. But this last tree has no one there: he has come back from the dead for us Nathaniels to follow: and to come home with us—like Zacchaeus.

Past, present, future: will we let Jesus be there?

10.2 Run to Win!

Bible references: Romans 13:14; Philippians 3:14; 2 Timothy 4:7–8; Hebrews 12:2.

Audience: Children; sports people.

Aim: To use sporting activities as a parable for joining and living the Christian life.

Visual aids: Lots of pictures/acetates are needed, indicated throughout the Outline (VA = visual aid). Make sure they are big enough to be seen. Real photos, good drawings or cartoons will all work. In 'The Champion' section, aim to get the champ and the risen Jesus looking identical, apart from clothing and nailprints.

Handy hint: A lot of material, so hurry through, or give the talk over a few sessions.

Outline: Say how your life is like a multi-event sports competition. Who will win? (VA, starter with gun.) God gets us going (expand each point as you wish). He has given good rules to enable a clean race. Alas! We have failed. (VA, pole vaulter/high jumper knocking bar off.) Share one or two ways this has happened.

But, there is a Champion. (VA, bearded winner, arms

150

aloft, running vest, on podium.) The winner is—(VA, Jesus, arms aloft, outside empty tomb, nailprints) Jesus! Talk of how he beat sin on the cross (the nailprints), and death by being raised. He can be our Champion.

We must join his team. (VA, runner, vest has cross as badge.) Explain the badge. (VA, cross.) It cost Jesus everything: that is the best reason for wearing it. As a team member, there will be training. (VA, gym, weights, push-ups.) Everyone will see us. (VA, grandstand—some happy, some angry.)

To succeed, we need to feed well (VA, athlete eating steak) on God's word, and breathe in his Holy Spirit. (VA, swimmer turning for breath.) We want to win. (VA, athlete breasts tape.) We look to Jesus (Hebrews 12:2), aiming for the crown (2 Timothy 4:7–8). We press on for the prize (Philippians 3:14).

What a lot to say! Whatever you leave out (or deal with another day), lead towards how we *join*. The life from Jesus is ready. (VA, track suit with cross badge, hanging up.) We must put it on. (VA, athlete putting on track suit from previous VA.) You could use Romans 13:14.

If you have the balance of how great, and how hard, being a Christian is, you can call for a response.

10.3 The Why and the How

Bible references: Psalm 51:3; Isaiah 6:8; 59:2; Jeremiah 1:7; Mark 5:19; 9:24; John 8:34, 36; 10:10; Acts 2:21; Philippians 2:5–8; 1 John 5:12.

Audience: Children; family services.

Aim: To show very simply why and how we become Christians.

Visual aids: Six pictures/acetates: 1. A person bowed down with sin, away from God. 2. A simple cross. 3. Several people of varied ages. 4. The person kneeling at the cross (VA 1 and 2). 5. The person (VA 1) standing, as the cross (VA 2) invades the sin of VA 1. 6. A pair of hands, empty, and open to receive.

Outline: Did you get this talk from the visual aids? Explain how you became a Christian—for whatever reason, but how you now realise there were three reasons: 1. For yourself (VA 1). Admit that, like most people, you are selfish—so self first! How sad that sin (explain it simply— the good we don't do, and the wrong we do do) cuts us off from God (Isaiah 59:2), takes our life (1 John 5:12, second half), and spoils us (John 8:34). Say how you wanted to get rid of it!

Your second (main?) reason for becoming a Christian was for Christ's sake (VA 2). You may want to run through Philippians 2:5–8 to show how much Jesus gave, and how that love drew you. Thirdly (VA 3), others need you to be a Christian, because you have to share the love of Jesus with them (Isaiah 6:8). Jeremiah 1:7 is lovely for children, as is Mark 5:19 for parents and children.

Hopefully you have your audience with you, and they want to know 'How?' by this stage. Again, three things—three steps: Step 1, admit our need (VA 4). David's Psalm 51:3 is good. Say how even you can get this far! Step 2, accept (VA 5). Jesus brings new life, not us (John 10:10): he sets us free (John 8:36). The lovely response of the father in Mark 9:24 will touch parents here.

Which brings you to VA 6. Say how these are like your hands, as Step 3 is—ask. Acts 2:21 is helpful: we have to ask Jesus. When the author of this book became a Christian as a boy, he said to his mother, 'I want Jesus to be my Saviour.' To which she replied, 'Then you must ask him.' And he did.

Children can ask Jesus: he will give them his eternal life.

10.4 *Which Way?*

Bible references: Genesis 3:8; Psalm 14:3; Isaiah 30:21; 53:6; 55:6–7; 59:2; Micah 6:8; Mark 1:17; John 3:16; 14:6; Romans 7:19.

Audience: Children; young people; families.

Aim: To show the way to God, via Jesus.

Visual aids: A series of pictures/acetates:

1. *No Stopping* road sign. Could have a person walking, with signpost 'To God'.
2. *No Turning* sign. Could have person standing at double 'To God/To My Way' sign.
3. *No Entry* sign. Could have road with huge chasm, person unable to cross.
4. *No Waiting* sign. Could have chasm of last picture bridged by cross (the more dramatic the better).
   (VA = visual aid.)

Outline: Explain how life is a sort of journey: VA 1. God wants us to walk with him (Micah 6:8). The first half of Genesis 3:8 is a lovely picture of this. God will help us to do it (Isaiah 30:21). Jesus wants us to go with him (Mark

154

1:17): he is the way (John 14:6). Say how wonderful this way is, with an anecdote or two from your life.

Which way did we choose (VA 2)? We went astray (Psalm 14:3), going our own way (Isaiah 53:6), even when we didn't want to (Romans 7:19). We did not live as friends of God (the second half of Genesis 3:8). Own up to your own going away from God, identifying with your audience.

Which leads to our being cut off from God (VA 3) (Isaiah 59:2). Don't dwell on this too long, but get across the sadness of it—from our side and God's: he misses us, too. That will lead to the answer, and the way back (VA 4). God rebuilds the road. It costs his Son's life: show how special and wonderful that is (John 3:16), and why John 14:6 fits this part of the journey, too.

Isaiah 55:6–7 are lovely verses to paraphrase in a simple way for a younger audience, to invite them to 'return'.

10.5 My Big Brother

Bible references: Mark 3:31–35; John 20:17; Romans 8:29; Hebrews 2:11–12.

Audience: Children; young people; families.

Aim: To encourage youngsters especially to let Jesus be permanent 'family'.

Illustrations: Happy and positive examples from your own life will be good. Equally, contrasting examples between how things may not have worked out in your childhood, compared with the help Jesus gives will help. Try not to embarrass your family with your stories!

Outline: If you have a good family story of how someone saved your/your sibling's life, it will make a great introduction: 'When I was five, I fell in a swamp, and my big brother crawled across and . . . .' Or you could say how you wish you had someone in your family who was always there—to be wise, to talk with, laugh and cry with.

Good news! Jesus can be the perfect big brother. How? He was born before us, to be our brother (Romans 8:29). He lived as we should do. He died for us. Talk about John Newton, once a slave owner, author of 'How sweet the name of Jesus sounds'. In that hymn, he wrote a line,

'Jesus, my Shepherd, Brother, Friend.' But in most hymn books now, the line reads 'Jesus, my Shepherd, Saviour, Friend.' 'Brother' has become 'Saviour': draw the analogy: that is what really happened. Don't be afraid to speak simply and movingly about the death of Jesus to children. His love will mean a great deal to them, if spoken of sensitively.

When Jesus rose, was he going to be angry with the disciples for their having run away? Of course not: he called them 'my brothers' (John 20:17). When we come and give our lives to him, he calls us brothers, too (Hebrews 2:11–12). As we live the life he wants us to, we are his brothers and sisters (Mark 3:31–35).

It's time for Jesus to be the big brother, as we share in his family. Gently invite children (and older folk, too) to meet him.

11. A Family Affair

With an increasing concern for family life, there is a great opportunity presented for sharing the good news with those who are married, or living together in a permanent relationship.

11.1 God's Greatest Gifts

Bible reading: Genesis 2:4–7, 18–24. Also Genesis 1:28; 3:8; John 8:34, 36; 10:10; Romans 5:5; 1 John 4:16; Revelation 3:20.

Audience: Weddings; family gatherings; parents/marrieds evenings.

Aim: To show from Genesis that marriage and family life are God's gifts to us; so let's not leave him out.

Outline: Ask what is the best wedding present/best thing about the marriage/family. The best gift/things have been given by the maker of marriages and families: God himself. What does he give us?

Life. Genesis 2:7. God made everything to be 'good' (all through Genesis 1), but one thing was not good (2:18): it is good to be together (2:24). Alas, we left God out, and often get it wrong. Explain how this is true of you since you got married. Jesus comes to die for our sins, and brings a brilliant new life (John 10:10). Ask if your audience is going it alone, or letting the giver of life bring them his life.

His life is not dreadful, for we have *liberty* to enjoy it, and be successful (1:28). Sadly, we became slaves (John

8:34). Jean-Jacques Rousseau (*'Le Contrat Social'*) said, 'Man was born free, and everywhere he is in chains.' Jesus comes to return us to liberty (John 8:36), to stop us/rescue us from the wrong. Will we receive his freedom into our marriages/families?

Best of all, *love*. 'God is love' (1 John 4:16). Paint the lovely picture of God walking with the first couple in their garden (3:8), and the desperate tragedy of their hiding. Explain how his love sent his Son to the cross and, by his Holy Spirit, that love can be in our hearts once again (Romans 5:5). He stands at the door of our hearts and homes, waiting to come in (Revelation 3:20). Will we let him enter, with his life, liberty and love—the greatest gifts?

11.2 Feel the Difference!

Bible reading: John 2:1–11. Also Psalm 34:8; Romans 3:23.

Audience: Weddings; married people; families.

Aim: To show, from the wedding at Cana, the splendid difference Jesus makes to our lives.

Outline: In a general situation, ask why Christians get so excited, and say it is because Jesus makes all the difference in the world. In a wedding/marriage/family talk, start with how wonderful marriage is, and how brilliant if we let Jesus share it (v.2). Give testimony to your own situation, if you can speak of your Christian marriage. Ask if your hearers have ever let Jesus share their lives, marriages, work, homes and families.

A little levity now about the wine (v.3), especially as older versions translate 'The wine failed'—hardly its fault! They had wanted a perfect wedding, but got the wine wrong. Show how we all want perfect lives, but fall short of God's perfect standard (Romans 3:23)—and our own expectations, too. Who has the answer, when we don't get life right?

Say that some excellent advice was given by Mary

162

(v.5)—to do as Jesus said. Who will be wise enough to hear her? Who influences us? His answer seemed crazy: the jars (v.6) held 1,000 bottles of water (what a wine festival!). Say that we know it will be wine: but we look with hindsight. For the servants, they put their lives on the line, as the man in charge says, 'Ah: Lake Galilee, AD 30—excellent water.' End of job for servants! To trust Jesus still takes courage, as everyone sees.

But the miracle (v.9) produces the best (v.10). Three years later, you can explain, Jesus took the wine of his blood to give the best for us—forgiveness through his death and new life from the resurrection: the sparkling wine of the Holy Spirit.

At this wedding/in your family (apply to your hearers), Jesus wants the best for you. Psalm 34:8: 'Taste and see that the Lord is good' is a lovely invitation with which to end.

11.3 But God . . . .

Bible passage: 1 Samuel 3:1–10. Also 2:22; 3:19–21; Judges 21:25; Leviticus 24:2; John 1:5, 29; 8:12; Ephesians 2:8–9; Hebrews 10:19–22; Revelation 22:16.

Audience: Parents; teachers; family services.

Aim: To show that we have problems, but God has the big answers.

Outline: Problems, problems! Say how life is full of them. Yes—but God . . . .. Explain that you want to show God's answers using one of the best loved Bible incidents about a boy called Samuel. Sketch in the background from 1 Samuel 1 and 2 very quickly, as to how he came to be in the Temple.

Problem one. God's voice was rarely heard (v.1). Everyone did their own thing (Judges 21:25), even the High Priest's family was off the rails (2:22). But the light still burned (v.3), as it always had (Leviticus 24:2). Talk about this world seeming dark with evil, and how like the Judges verse we are today (give a couple of instances). But God's light is here (John 1:5): Jesus (John 8:12). As the Temple light went out at dawn, the 'morning star' is coming (Revelation 22:16). Will we let Jesus be the light in our darkness?

Problem two puts the problem in reverse: Samuel lived a good life, but did not know God. He worked in the Temple (v.3), and ministered (v.1): yet verse 7 shows his need. Talk about our need for God to speak to us, and change us through Jesus: you could use Ephesians 2:8–9.

Samuel did not recognise God (*problem three*) when he called (v.5). But Eli pointed the way (v.9); just as John the Baptist pointed people to Jesus (John 1:29). Jesus is now our way to God. Unpack Hebrews 10:19–22, to show how his life, death and resurrection give us the 'Way In'.

Problem four is a great encouragement with which to end, and inspire your hearers. Samuel does not know what to say—but God comes anyway. Samuel only has seven words to remember (v.9). He manages to miss out a key one (v.10); but God still speaks (v.11), and it is the start of a lifetime relationship (vv. 19, 21).

Say how we may feel ignorant, far away, small, unable to pray: but God will come to be real to us. We only need to let him.

11.4 Back to Childhood

Bible references: Matthew 18:3–4; John 3:7; 8:36; Romans 5:5; Hebrews 12:7; 1 Peter 5:7.

Audience: Parents and teachers.

Aim: To take Matthew 18:3, and show what becoming like a little child means as a picture of becoming a Christian.

Handy hint: As with other talks in this section, try not to embarrass your family with personal reminiscences that are too intimate!

Outline: Begin with a personal story or two of how much children need to know: from your own childhood, or questions you have been asked. Explain how Jesus says a very odd thing: to become Christians, we have to learn from children, rather than vice versa (Matthew 18:3).

Ask what children have that we need. How are they pictures of God's children? Here are some ideas (you may not have time for them all).

Family. Say how sad family breakdown is, because children need stability. How amazing that God is Father: we can have an everlasting family with him. Speak of how much this means to you, as an adult.

Trust. No one trusts like a small child—give a simple example. Whom can we trust? 1 Peter 5:7 is a lovely verse.

Freedom. Who dances bare in your lounge?! Answer: the three-year-old after a bath (not Mummy!). Children enjoy a freedom like no one else. Yet they are limited too. Compare John 8:36 and Hebrews 12:7, where Jesus sets us free, but disciplines us. Say what a special freedom this is for you.

Humility. Children know their limitations (Matthew 18:4). Jesus brings a realism to our lives.

Learning. Like children, God's Spirit will teach us.

Forgiveness. This, and the next, are probably the ones to major on. Children know the need to be forgiven, and also forgive readily. A couple of simple stories would go well here, leading up to how God forgives us—and helps us do the same. Speak of the cross, and how much we need that help.

Love. Children receive and give love generously. Romans 5:5 speaks of both God's love and his Holy Spirit.

Get back to the first bit of Matthew 18:3: 'Repent, change, turn about' (Amplified): as radical as birth (John 3:7). Invite your hearers to become children—God's children.

11.5 Let's Play Mums and Dads

Bible passage: Mark 10:13–16. Also refer to Genesis 1:28; Proverbs 22:6; Isaiah 49:16.

Audience: Parents, teachers. Needs careful adaptation but can be used when children present (eg family services).

Aim: To encourage parents to establish Christian homes and families by giving a positive lead as Christians themselves.

Handy hint: You are bound to draw on personal family stories. Make sure your partner and children will be able to show their faces again! If speaking of other families, get their permission or make them very anonymous. Having said that, it is good to scatter personal stories of successes and failures with God in your family all through the talk. You will manage best if you do not claim to be the perfect parent!

Outline: Having children seemed a good idea at the time! But young people today . . . A jokey introduction is good. What about a quote such as, 'They have execrable manners, flout authority, have no respect for their elders. What kind of awful creatures will they be when they grow up?' Who said it? Socrates, fourth century BC!

How can we help today's children? Good news! God wants to be in it with us, with his blessings. You could read the Mark verses here. Show that the disciples are typical of many: compare with Jesus in verse 14. Jesus is the fulfilment of Isaiah 49:16, as he died for our children, and us. He wants to bless us as families. Brother Lawrence said: 'We have a God who is infinitely gracious, and knows all our wants.' You might interject stories of times when you have been glad of God's blessings and presence in your family. (A child being sick at 3am; Monday mornings; joys and griefs; God's forgiveness when you have got it wrong.)

Because God has wanted to bless us from day one (Genesis 1:28), and will do so now (v.16), we must bring our children to him (v.13). That is God's command (Proverbs 22:6). Remind your hearers of those who say: 'I just let him make up his own mind,' and question if those parents really give choice, eg if they never go with them to church, how does a child know that is an option?

End with, 'What about verse 15?' If ever we needed God's help, it is now. Say how glad you are that God has your family: commend your hearers to take him home with them.

12. Home Helps

Some talks work best in small gatherings, for example at a coffee morning, tea party or dinner in someone's home. A few neighbours or friends are invited—but how can we speak in a non-preaching style?

The following are some suggestions which may enable the speaker to 'chat' the talk, possibly with an ending which gives room for come-back and questions.

12.1 Our Father

Bible references: Matthew 6:9–15; Luke 11:1–4.

Audience: Anybody. Will work in a very small setting; a church; with an older age group; people with little knowledge of God. Adapt as necessary.

Aim: To go through each section of the Lord's Prayer, highlighting the impact on our lives so that, by the end, the listeners may enter into a personal family relationship with 'Our Father'.

Visual aid: Get a beautifully designed enlarged version of the Lord's Prayer to show. Or use an overhead projector to reveal each part of the prayer as you come to it.

Handy hints: This is a quiet talk! Use a 'we' rather than a 'you' style. Give people a silent time to respond at the end.

Outline: Get a good illustration of an over-complicated way of saying something: a Government directive, for example. Compare it with your relief at being able to talk with God in fewer than seventy words in which you can include everything from his eternal greatness to your bread-and-butter needs. How? In a prayer we all know: quote the Lord's Prayer.

Take it phrase by phrase, showing briefly what each means. Francis of Assisi rarely got past the first two words, overcome by what he had already said. Speak of the wonder of a family relationship with the God 'in heaven', and of his ambition to bring us there. Then give the balance that he is 'hallowed'—holy, and to be worshipped. How wonderful if we could have heaven on earth. Give a couple of up-to-the-minute examples where God's love and peace would bless our world: 'Thy kingdom come. . . .'

Joke about sandwiches: you bother less with the outside than with the yummy filling, yet God bothers about our 'daily bread'. Now for your climax: show how we have failed to let God be Father, ignored heaven, not put him first, built our own kingdoms, made our own bread. That is why we need 'Forgive us'. And he will. The only person who did not need the Lord's Prayer was its Author. Speak of the cross, where he said 'Forgive *them*.' We can and must receive this and, when we do, the comparatively small sins against us will be easier to forgive.

Conclude with the wonder of God's Holy Spirit giving us a new life and victory over 'temptation' and 'evil'. Have you examples in your own life? God can do it—he has 'the power'—and we give him glory! You could ask for a silent saying of the prayer with real meaning at the end.

12.2 Room for You

Bible passage: John 14:1–6.

Audience: A small gathering. Would be helpful for the elderly or the bereaved.

Aim: To help people move in to God's kingdom via the only way there is.

Visual aids: A saw, a set square, a hammer and chisel, a paste-board and brush.

Outline: What about an enthusiastic opening? 'I want to talk about heaven!' Or produce the building and decorating equipment, reminiscing about your successes (even better, your failures!) at home-making. Either start will get you into the words of Jesus at the end of verse 2.

Go back to your decorating. You went to get the ladder from the shed, the brushes from the loft, the paint from the garage. Where did Jesus go 'to prepare a place for you'? Within twenty-four hours he would be on a cross, buying salvation with wood and nails. By Sunday morning he was back from the dead—with the rock from the tomb, and a new life for himself and us. Finally he went back with everything needed to get heaven ready. Try and develop the preparing and building theme.

Move on from the place to the people: if the rooms are getting prepared, are we? 'A place for *you*.' How are we fixed? Work through verse 6. Are we going via Jesus, trusting him as the truth, receiving the life of his Holy Spirit? Develop this as you have time, and as appropriate to the audience.

For a younger group, you may want to show how much a positive reaction cost the first disciples, including Thomas (v.5). They had long, tough journeys on their way home to their rooms. However hard, who wants to miss heaven? Let's go!

For any audience: heaven mattered enough to Jesus for him to die to buy it. Will we take the room prepared for us?

12.3 Give Me Your Heart

Bible references: Proverbs 21:2; 23:26; Jeremiah 17:9–10; Mark 7:21–23; Matthew 22:37; 27:46; Psalm 51:6.

Audience: Small gatherings; open-air metings; when a short talk is needed.

Aim: To show that Christ wants our hearts, the very centre of our lives.

Visual aid: Some portable bathroom scales.

Outline: As an opener, talk about how you cannot fool your doctor about your health, because he can find the truth. That is the way it is with God and the 'real you'. Or talk about a recent excess of eating which means you are not friends with the bathroom scales. In either case, make the opening personal and with an amusing anecdote.

Then explain how we all have a health/weight problem because 'The Lord weighs the heart' (Proverbs 21:2). You could show where it is in the Bible, if you intend to flick the page for the other key verse, below. Talk about how we come to be overweight, using such verses as Jeremiah 17:9–10 or Mark 7:21–23. Make it personal, or it will be 'holier than thou'. Show how our sins separate us from a holy God. Then bring in Matthew 27:46, where Jesus carries the weight of our sin as he is separated from God for us.

Now you can flick the page to Proverbs 23:26, 'My son, give me your heart.' We give the very centre of our lives to the Saviour who loves us, enabling verses like Psalm 51:6 and Matthew 22:37 to come true, because Jesus gives us his new life in our hearts.

End by saying that your bathroom scales may need you to do something, but God's scales are looking good, because Jesus tips the scales to make them right. You could say how that happened and is happening for you, as you invite your listeners to open their lives for Jesus to make all the difference.

12.4 What a Lovely Wash!

Bible references: 2 Kings 5:1–14; Job 15:14; Psalm 51:7; Isaiah 1:18; 6:5; 44:22; 64:6; Mark 1:40–42; 7:1–23; 1 John 1:7.

Audience: Small groups; ladies; older people.

Aim: To show how Jesus can cleanse our lives.

Handy hint: This Outline has several good stories. People love people-pictures: keep them moving, and alive. Don't over-elaborate any one of them, or the talk will drag, and take too long.

Outline: A homely opening is always good—some recent story involving household cleanliness would help (a blocked drain, a dog disaster, a lovely bath). The old saying goes 'Cleanliness is next to godliness.' The first is possible—but the second?

Explain the problem. Don't detail Mark 7:1–23, but précis quickly, centring on verses 21–23: we do do wrong things. Isaiah 6:5 and 64:6 lead to that key Old Testament question in Job 15:14: 'What is man, that he could be pure?'

A lovely story provides a picture answer: the leper's cleansing in Mark 1:40–42. Only a touch, and a life is

changed, echoes of 1 John 1:7. The man's plea parallels
David's prayer in Psalm 51:7, and his new skin is like
Isaiah 1:18 for our hearts. Sir Marcus Loane (ex-
Archbishop of Australia) said, 'Men's sins are buried in
the depth of the sea, and if they are buried by God they
will not be washed up on the shore.' For another picture,
Isaiah 44:22 is lovely.

If you have time, the story of Naaman in 2 Kings 5:1–14
is a splendid way to show how the washing can happen, as
we lose our pride and do as God says, with the great result
of verse 14. Invite your hearers to come, as they are, to the
Jesus whose blood will cleanse them, and whose Spirit
will make them new.

12.5 *He Has the Right*

Bible passage: Mark 2. Also Matthew 7:29.

Audience: Small home meetings; church services (the reading would be Mark 2:1–12); sceptics.

Aim: To show that Jesus has the right to claim our allegiance.

Handy hint: Although the talk is a walk-through of Mark 2, it is better to talk about what happens there, rather than read it, if speaking in someone's home, or it will seem too much like a lesson and sermon in church.

Outline: Start with some topical reference to other faiths ('Don't all roads lead to God?' 'What about Muslims in our schools?' 'What about these modern-day religious wars?'). So who does Jesus think he is? He 'taught with authority' (Matthew 7:29). What authority?

Show how that has always been the question, as Jesus lived with another faith—the Jewish. Tell the story in Mark 2:1–12 as the dramatic, funny, controversial story it is: the men, their friend, the crowd, the roof, and the shock of what Jesus said. Explain his proof—by healing the man, and how his cross and resurrection are so vital for us, and all the world. 'Who can forgive sins?' (v.7). Jesus has the right to forgive us. That is no threat, it is wonderful! Ask if your audience has let him, and give testimony as to what his forgiveness means in your life.

You could stop here, or go on to the two consequences of this right to forgive. From verses 13 to 17, Jesus has the right to call Levi (Matthew) and us to 'Follow me' (v.14). The one who forgives is alive: will we go with him? Talk about how he has called you. In verses 18 to 27, Jesus gives a new way of living. The good thing is that both incidents indicate positive, exciting, non-legalistic behaviour. Say how Jesus takes boredom out of life. 'Thou shalt not' is not your experience! His way may mean the opposition is vocal (vv. 18, 24), but the way is good.

You might like to end along the lines of, 'Here we are in this lovely home. We didn't come in via the roof! But Jesus is here. Who will go home with him?'

13. Charming Churchgoers

The church was never intended to be a 'closed shop'. Within every church should be those who are coming to faith, and would appreciate help in getting there. Others may lack assurance, or have mistaken ideas as to what it means to be a Christian. Here are some outlines for those who, though being fairly consistent in church attendance, do not have a real heart relationship with God.

13.1 All Change

Bible reading: Revelation 3:14–22. Also Malachi 3:10; Luke 12:21; 2 Corinthians 8:9; Revelation 7:13–14.

Audience: Primarily church folk; 'respectable' people!

Aim: To show how vital it is for Jesus Christ to change our lives.

Handy hint: The Bible passage paints brilliant verbal pictures: try and do the same. Some background reading about Laodicea will help, especially the geography, and activities in the first century.

Outline: Talk about a major change in your life which was painful but necessary. A fun one would be good—there is some serious stuff to follow.

Paint the picture of the hot springs at Hierapolis on the hill, piped down to Laodicea for first-century central heating—but arriving lukewarm, and thus useless. Our lives should be hot for God, with sin frozen out; but the hot got colder and the cold got warmer. We need to be changed.

Laodicea was a banking centre. Were the churchgoers relying on their wealth (v.17)? Remember Jesus speaking of a man who was not 'rich towards God' (Luke 12:21)?

Are we receiving God's gifts (as in Malachi 3:10, for example)?

Here is a question: what will you wear in heaven? Give a few silly/serious suggestions (eg, robes worn in church; jeans and T-shirt). Some in the Laodicean church would have been makers of woollen clothes—the town was famous for them. But they are 'naked' (v.17), and God will clothe them (v.18—and see Revelation 7:13–14). We need this, too. Only God can equip us for heaven.

If there is time, talk about the Holy Spirit opening our eyes (end of verse 18). If not, get to verse 20 (get there whatever else you miss!). Here is the lonely traveller, at the end of the day, coming to our house: he has bought us all we need (see 2 Corinthians 8:9). Will we let him in?

13.2 How Did You Get In?

Bible reading: John 10:1–11. Also John 10:12–18, 27–30; 14:6.

Audience: People who need to understand the true way into God's kingdom.

Aim: To explain that Jesus is the way, and why, using John 10 as a basis.

Outline: 'If you claim to be a Christian, how did you get in?' This is known as a 'head-butting' opening! Alternatively . . . one of the loveliest pictures of Jesus is as the Good Shepherd in John 10; let us see how it helps us understand the way we start as Christians. A personal anecdote about mistaken ideas you or others have had about what is a Christian may be good. A teenager said, 'A Christian is someone who grows his own vegetables'— true story!

You need to get to verses 7 and 9, 'I am the gate' ('door' in some translations). There is only one way to God (John 14:6). Why? He paid the entrance fee (vv.11, 15). He was the volunteer (v.18). Make it sound very wonderful (which it is): especially as he is now looking for us (v.16).

A gate (door) has two sides. Describe both. First, outside (good to put the bad news first, and go towards the positive). The devil is there, ruining everything (first part of v.10). People trying to get in without Jesus are there, too (v.1). You need to challenge your audience whether they are claiming their way is right (doing their best, being good church members) and so stealing God's right to *give* new life, and heaven. If you have time, verses 12 and 13 speak of bad shepherds, leading astray.

Inside the gate, we are saved (v.9) from that evil, and wrong ways. We have new life. Alan Dale's paraphrase of verse 10 says, 'I came to help people to live, and to live splendidly.' Jesus keeps us (v.9) for always (v.28). He knows us (vv.14, 27) and we know him (v.3) and follow him (v.4), listening to his voice (v.27). We are identified as part of the 'flock' (v.16). Pick your favourites and show how great they are, with some personal testimony.

Now invite your audience to come on in via Jesus, as they give themselves to him.

13.3 Let's Go!

Bible reading: Hosea 5:13–6:3. Also Genesis 3:23–24; Exodus 3:14; Isaiah 1:5–6, 18; Ezekiel 18:4, 20; 33:11; Micah 6:8; Romans 6:23; Matthew 11:28; 22:4; John 7:37–38; 8:34; Luke 15:5; Ephesians 5:18; 1 John 1:7.

Audience: Churchgoers; those who feel far from God (in prison, for example).

Aim: To show the huge need for, and wonderful results of, turning to God with our whole lives.

Outline: This is one of those rare occasions where a dramatic reading of some Bible verses makes a great introduction. Simply read Hosea 6:1–3, with or without a preliminary explanation. Then say how brilliant you think these verses are.

Did your audience see the *great contrast*? On the one side is 'the Lord' (v.1), a name of power (you could refer to the ultimate name 'I am' in Exodus 3:14). Verse 3 starts with how safe and certain God is. Corrie ten Boom said, 'God has no problems, only plans. There is no panic in Heaven.' You can use the start of verse 2 to talk of the cross and resurrection ('the third day'), and God's love, and life. On the other hand: us. We are 'torn' (v.1; see

Isaiah 1:5–6), by God: sent from him because of our sin (Genesis 3:23–24). We are 'injured' (v.1), as in John 8:34. As we need to be revived (v.2), there are echoes of Romans 6:23 and Ezekiel 18:4 and 20.

Tell them what a relief, with such a contrast, to hear the *great call* at the start of verses 1 and 3. You could major on the 'come' of verse 1, referring to Isaiah 1:18 and Matthew 11:28 and 22:4. Show how the invitation is to trust, not try.

So what if we respond? Enthuse over the *great consequence*: five-fold splendour!

1. '*He will heal us*' (v.1): our sin dealt with (1 John 1:7).

2. '*He will bind up our wounds*' (v.1). Have you an incident when you were cut, and your injury was bound up to make it well? Luke 15:5 could fit here.

3. '*He will revive us*' (v.2). Speak of the power of the Holy Spirit breathing in new life (Ephesians 5:18).

4. '*He will restore us*' (v.2). The new life being the one God always wanted for us (Micah 6:8). If you have a garden, the final one should give you scope for illustrations.

5. '*The refreshing*' of verse 3, as in John 7:37–38. We need God constantly showering our lives: talk of how he does this for you.

Wrap it up with the start of verse 1, echoing Ezekiel 33:11.

13.4 Can I Help You?

Bible reading: Matthew 20:29–34.

Audience: Church congregations; Palm Sunday.

Aim: To show that it is more what Jesus does for us, than what we do for him, that matters.

Outline: One way to start is to talk about life being a tough journey sometimes. We can make our own way, or let Jesus travel with us: he understands hard roads. Matthew 20:29 has him leaving Jericho, en route for Jerusalem, up 3,000 feet, over seventeen miles, towards a donkey (see 21:1–2), and a cross. Another beginning is to speak of an 'opportunity of a lifetime' being presented: here comes one in Matthew 20:29–34. Jesus is the giver: will we be like the two men who meet him?

Blind men by the roadside were 'nobodies'. Most of us feel we are not terribly important. But when they cried out, 'Jesus stopped' (v.32). They didn't let the crowd put them off (v.31). Are we afraid of others, as they get between us and Jesus? We learn to keep quiet as we get older, to be 'respectable'. Oliver Howarth (of Warwick University) said: 'The trouble with grown-ups is they can be too sensible for their own good.'

Explain that you often fall into the trap of thinking that Christianity is saying, 'What does God want me to do?' It becomes work and effort. What a shock to hear Jesus' question in verse 32. Isn't it brilliant? Ask your audience what they would answer if Jesus asked them. Do they need forgiveness? Or help? Or new life? Or the power of God's Holy Spirit? Or freedom from something which binds them? Dare they ask?

And what if they do? Show the two things which happened for those men in verse 34: first 'they received their sight'. Jesus will say 'Yes' to any of those questions in the previous paragraph. Second, they 'followed him'—seventeen miles and up 3,000 feet. Easier to stay sitting in Jericho, but better to go with Jesus. Will we take his hard road, with a new life?

You could end with: 'The saddest people here are those who, when Jesus asks, "What do you want me to do for you?" have no answer.' Suggest a simple prayer of response, to enable those who want to receive forgiveness and new life to do so.

13.5 The Man at the Gate

Bible reading: Acts 3:1–10. Also Mark 3:17; Luke 9:51–56; Acts 2:1–4.

Audience: Any church congregation.

Aim: To show that, however close we get to God, we need Jesus to change our lives.

Handy hint: This is a good story (and true). Tell it as such, making the characters live.

Outline: Have you read a complicated book/seen an obscurely plotted play or film recently? Say how hard it was to follow what was what and who was who. Today is different: a good story, and easy to follow: read Acts 3:1–10 here, if it has not come earlier in the meeting.

Talk about the three *dramatis personae* (theatre talk for those taking part!). The first two (v.1)—we even call children after them—are great Christian leaders. Explain how they were not always like that: instance what they once were. You could talk of Peter the big-head (walking on water, saying he would not desert or deny Jesus) who also failed (he fell in, ran away, denied). John was a tough guy ('Son of Thunder' Mark 3:17), and nasty with it (as in his reaction to the Samaritans in Luke 9:51–56). Now, in

Acts 3, they are new: you could talk of Acts 2:1–4, and the Holy Spirit coming.

Introduce character three: the lame man (v.2), a picture of the crippling effect of sin on us: we limp through life. He asked for too little (v.2). Older translations say 'he asked for alms': but he didn't need alms, he needed legs! (Sorry!) Say how we ask for too little (money, car, house, nice family). We need a new life, forgiveness, heaven. If you want to, say that the people going to church only gave money: why? Ask the Christians if we only meet material needs, or give more—the offer of God's Spirit?

Joke about two big fishermen saying they have no money (v.6): thanks a lot! Then, the one word he needed: 'Walk'. Say how Jesus reaches out with his hand to us, saying 'Live'. Talk of the nail-mark on it: he has paid, and is back from the dead. Verse 8 gives the balance of the joy, and everyone seeing: we have those things when Jesus changes us.

End with an invitation to reach out to Jesus. For older audiences, the words spoken by King George VI in his pre-Second World War Christmas broadcast would go well (written by Minnie Haskins):

> I said to the man who stood at the gate of the year, 'Give me a light, that I may tread safely into the unknown.' And he replied, 'Go out into the darkness, and put your hand into the hand of God; that will be for you better than light and safer than a known way.'

13.6 How Are You?

Bible passage: John 11:1–17, 34–44. Also Matthew 28:19; Galatians 2:20; Ephesians 2:1; John 1:8–9.

Audience: Soporific churchgoers!

Aim: To enliven those who claim to be Christians, but have fallen by the wayside.

Handy hint: Don't be too heavy!

Outline: Relate an incident when you fooled everyone you were fine, but your doctor told you the truth, because he knew. Explain that Jesus is the one we can't kid. As you are going to speak of Lazarus' problems, emphasise John 11:5: Jesus loved him, as he does us. His concern is in verse 35, as for us in Galatians 2:20. What impact does that have on us? Lazarus did not react for several reasons. Are we suffering from his symptoms?

Symptom one: *asleep* (v.11). Have we nodded off? Sleepers are unaware of the world around them. Is our church like that? Have we forgotten Matthew 28:19? Dr C.V. Hill said, 'We must be fishers of men, not keepers of the aquarium.' Ask if Jesus needs to nudge us awake (as in v.11).

Symptom two: *in a tomb* (v.17). Admit how your Christianity sometimes feels in a rut, like a deep grave. Duncan Campbell said, 'Many a Christian worker has buried his spirituality in the grave of his activity.' Is our church boring? A child looked round his church and asked, 'Why is there no ceiling?'

'Be quiet!' came the reply.

'No carpet?'

'Be quiet.'

'Why is it cold?'

'Be quiet.'

'Why?'

'Because it's God's house.'

'Well, if I were God, I'd move.'

Third symptom: *behind a stone* (v.38). Share how you sometimes face problems which seem impossible to move: you get stuck. Announce the good news at the start of verse 39.

Symptom four: *he stank!* Newer versions are more polite than the AV's 'He stinketh' (v.39)! Own up to how sin makes your life smell bad (1 John 1:8–9 was written to Christians).

Of course, Lazarus had an ultimate (fifth) symptom: *he was dead* (v.14)! He needed verses 43 and 44, as we need Ephesians 2:1. Only the death and resurrection of Jesus can bring us alive.

Finally, symptom six: *he was bound* (v.44), and Jesus freed him. Do we need the Holy Spirit to free us up? Howard Snyder said, 'The church has resurrection life within it. It needs only to be unbound and let go.'

Run through the six symptoms as a sum-up. Ask which ones were true: will we let Jesus be the good Doctor, and give the remedy?

14. A Few Festivals

Throughout this book are talks which can be used, or adapted, for the high days and holy days of the church's calendar. This section gives some specific suggestions for important days and dates, when faith-sharing is particularly appropriate.

14.1 A Gift—for God?

Bible references: Genesis 1:27; Psalm 8:4–5; Matthew 7:7; 10:8; 20:28; John 4:14; 14:16; Romans 8:32; 1 Corinthians 6:19–20; 15:57; 1 Timothy 6:17; James 1:5; 4:6; 1 Peter 1:18–19; 2 Peter 2:1; Jude 24.

Audience: Harvest, Christmas, Easter congregations; other events at those festivals, and other services generally (eg church birthdays).

Aim: To show how special we are to God, and how he wants us to belong to him.

Handy hint: This is a very adaptable talk. Bring in seasonal references, such as harvest offerings, Christmas presents, giving Easter eggs, as the theme develops about Jesus giving us to God, and God's gifts to us.

Outline: Introduce this topically, or seasonally, talking of wanting to give the best onions (harvest), egg (Easter), present (Christmas, birthday). Ask what people give. Have a few suggestions. If your hearers were Jesus, what would they give God this harvest/Christmas/ Easter? The best. What is that?

Look at your hearers: 'You are. You are the best.' Explain how the best of creation is humankind (Genesis

198

1:27, Psalm 8:4–5). Show how we got it wrong, went away, stopped being best: so Jesus came to buy us back, with his life and death (Matthew 20:28). Talk of the cost of presents, and then the cost of us (1 Peter 1:18–19). Now Jesus wants to present us to his Father (Jude 24). We can choose to say 'No' (2 Peter 2:1), and remain away. Or we can come (1 Corinthians 6:19–20).

Now turn the coin over. God has presents for us, too. Using Romans 8:32, pick your favourite gifts from God, enthuse about them, and give personal testimony as to their blessings in your life. Some you could mention are: everything (1 Timothy 6:17); grace and forgiveness (James 4:6); refreshment (John 4:14); the Holy Spirit (John 14:16); wisdom (James 1:5); victory (1 Corinthians 15:57). Two or three will do! Wrap them all up with a two-fold challenge: we need to ask, to receive (Matthew 7:7); and to share our gifts with others (Matthew 10:8).

Back to Part One, to ask who will be a gift *to* God, and into Part Two: who will receive *from* God? It is the present time for present time!

14.2 Presents for Christmas

Bible references: Luke 2:1–7. Plus John 14:2.

Audience: Any Christmas gathering.

Aim: To compare what we give to God with what he gives to us, and to encourage our heart response.

Visual aids: A shoe box full of hay, gift-wrapped. A clear bottle of coloured pop, nine-tenths drunk, gift wrapped. A purse, with a few coins in. A *huge* card, 'What can I give him?' on the front, big heart inside with the words 'Give him my heart' across top of inside.

Handy hints: This is a very visual Christmas talk. Make it live, as you open the visual aids. Have a big table plus at least two biros by the door, for the card to be signed. After speaking, 'In the bleak midwinter' might be appropriate.

Outline: Start by talking about the 'birthday boy': what shall we give him this year? Socks? Hankies? You have some presents with you!

A gift from home: beautifully wrapped box. Open to show hay, which you got from the garage/shed/rabbits/guinea pigs. You don't keep it in the house—not too close. Show how it has always been like that with Jesus, kept at arm's length: 'No room in the inn', and the hay of the manger (Luke 2:7). Yet he is preparing 'a place for you' in heaven (John 14:2). Won't we welcome him in to our 'inn' this Christmas?

Next—a gift for the birthday party. Produce the gift-wrapped bottle—almost all gone: you had some! Show how we give Jesus the left-overs—an odd moment on Christmas day. He gave all his time, from birth to death. Risen, he comes to ask to be involved all the time. Admit this is hard for you, but how wonderful, too.

Third, the purse. We give something (coins, even a note). He gave his whole life. Explain a little of the cross, and how he deserves all we are and have.

Now produce the huge card (big enough for many sig-natures). The big heart (bright colour—red?) shows what we can give. You might quote the last verse of 'In the bleak midwinter', commenting on the shepherd and wise man references, wrapping up with 'my heart'. Who will sign your card to him? Not just a signature—it means 'Yes' to him: it is on the table as they leave.

14.3 Fool!

Bible references: Psalm 14:1; Proverbs 12:15; 14:9; Isaiah 53:3; Ecclesiastes 2:14; Luke 4:33–34; 12:13–21; John 3:19; 12:35, 46; 1 Corinthians 1:18; 2 Timothy 3:15; 1 John 1:8–9.

Audience: April 1 meetings; young people; church services (Bible readings could be Psalm 14 and Luke 12:13–21).

Aim: With the word 'fool' as the theme, to show how we can become wise with God's salvation.

Handy hint: You may want to major on one or two of the fools in the outline, rather than tackling them all.

Outline: Have a good 'April fool' opening, or a story of when you made a fool of yourself, or someone called you a fool. Say how you felt, and that you don't want God to think you are one. As you have read your Bible you have been on the look-out for the people God calls fools.

The big one is in Psalm 14:1 (why is this the only Psalm repeated in its entirety twice—Psalm 53?): the fool who denies God's existence. Proofs of God's reality are in Talk 2.1. But even the evil spirits believe in God (Luke 4:33–34). Talk about how, even if we say we believe, we act as

202

if we do not, never thinking of him, speaking to him, living his way. We are fools, denying God.

Because of the wrong things we do, we choose to live away from God, as fools in the dark (Ecclesiastes 2:14). Jesus said the same in John 3:19, with the result in John 12:35. Say how glad you are that Jesus has come to light up your life (John 12:46).

That darkness includes everyone thinking their way is right (you could give some contrasting examples from the world of politics), but 'the way of a fool is right in his own eyes' (Proverbs 12:15). Jesus' story in Luke 18:9–14 is good here. 1 John 1:8–9 is a New Testament echo of Proverbs 14:9, 'Fools mock at making amends for sin.' All this leads to big danger, with the remarkable story in Luke 12:13–21, especially verse 20. Have you time to tell it dramatically, drawing the implication for us all?

People sometimes think Christians are fools. But we follow the one who was 'despised', and made a fool of (Isaiah 53:3). The cross is foolish to some, but it becomes God's power (1 Corinthians 1:18), and salvation makes us wise (2 Timothy 3:15). C.T. Studd, rich man and English cricketer, became a Christian and went to Ascot races. His top hat had 'I'm God's fool' on the front. As people stared after him, the back of the hat read, 'Whose fool are you?' It is a good story to end with, as you ask the same question!

14.4 Come to the Centre

Bible references: Lamentations 1:12; 3:22–27; Matthew 1:21; 27:32, 35, 44, 46, 51 (a reading could be 27:35–51); Luke 19:10; Galatians 2:20; Philippians 2:5–11; 3:10.

Audience: Good Friday, Lent and Holy Week congregations.

Aim: To show what the cross meant to Jesus, and means to us today.

Handy hint: You could give this as a pretend interview between you and Jesus, and then you and yourself, where you pose questions ('What was it like?') and answer in the first person.

Outline: George Macleod said, 'I am recovering the claim that Jesus was not crucified in a Cathedral between two candles, but on a cross between two thieves, on the town garbage heap . . . at the kind of place where cynics talk smut, thieves curse and soldiers gamble. Because that is where he died; and that is what he died about.'

You would like to ask Jesus, 'Why did you die?' Suggest some of the reasons people give for his death: 'To show God's love', 'To be an example'. Compare with Matthew 1:21, and what Jesus said in Luke 19:10. He

came, and died, 'to save'. Show how it cost him everything, using Matthew 27:32, 35, 44 and 46 and Philippians
2:5–8, speaking of the beatings, the pain, the loneliness,
and separation from his Father. However, it was worth it.
He opened the way to God (Matthew 27:51), and he was
raised triumphantly (Philippians 2:9–11).

And what does the cross mean to you? Back to Matthew
27:51: the way is open to God. Say how amazingly wonderful this is, with all that flows from this personal relationship. As it cost Jesus, explain how it costs you, too.
We are 'crucified with Christ' (Galatians 2:20), sharing
his sufferings (Philippians 3:10). This is especially tough
for young people (Lamentations 3:27).

Rejoice with your audience how the cross brings new
life: you could stick with Lamentations (a little-used
book), in 3:22–25. Similarly, 1:12 is a great challenge,
to wrap up the talk, as you invite people in their hearts to
kneel at the cross to trust the Christ who lives to bring his
life to us.

14.5 A Famous Victory

Bible readings: Matthew 28:1–10; 1 Corinthians 15:1–22. Also the rest of Matthew 28 and 1 Corinthians 15; Luke 24:13–35; John 20:15–16, 19, 27; 21:2–7, 15.

Audience: Easter services and meetings.

Aim: To celebrate Easter, and share its challenge to respond by taking and giving.

Handy hint: Capture the excitement, enthuse the response.

Outline: Open with the bigs of life—big breakfasts, big sporting games, big anniversaries. This is the big day for Christians. No Easter would mean no Christianity. This is Victory Day.

A victory to be *remembered*. Show how from day one the opposition has tried to avoid Jesus being risen (Matthew 28:11–15). But the evidence is all there. (A whole Outline [15.3] covers this.) Paul shows us in 1 Corinthians 15:3–8. Get excited about that chapter's verses 54–57, and the splendid finality of Matthew 28:2. 'Jesus Christ *is* risen today—Alleluia!'

Now ask if that is it: just a memory. No—this is a victory to be *received*. Pick your favourite Easter en-

counters, or kaleidoscope the personal meetings: the
women (Matthew 28:9); the Emmaus walk (Luke 24:13–
25); Mary (John 20:15–16); the disciples (John 20:19);
Thomas (John 20:27); the disciples (John 21:2–7); Peter
(John 21:15); Paul (1 Corinthians 15:8). Don't forget to
say how you have had a personal encounter with the risen
Christ: 'He lives within my heart.'

And then? Urge your audience not to be selfish and keep
this greatest news to themselves. It is a victory to be *re-
told*. Contrast the 'Come . . . see' of Matthew 28:6 with
'Go . . . tell' (v.7); and the urgency of 1 Corinthians
15:24. An Easter hymn says:

> Now he bids us tell abroad,
> How the lost may be restored,
> How the penitent forgiven,
> How we, too, may enter heaven.

You may make your challenge throughout the talk, as
you end each section. Or you may save it till here. Ask if
they believe it. Then they can receive it, by receiving the
risen Christ. And then—tell the world!

14.6 Meet the Master!

Bible reading: Revelation 1:4–18. Also 1 John 1:7; Revelation 22:20.

Audience: Easter and Ascension services.

Aim: To present the risen, glorified Christ, and enable people to meet him now.

Handy hint: The Revelation 1 passage is amazing. Try to capture something of its brilliance and paint its superb picture of Jesus. Soak it up yourself first!

Outline: 'If I could see Jesus, I'd believe!' Say that you have had that reaction from people, and the Bible does a great thing: it tells us what Jesus is like today, when we meet him. And/or a little Shakespeare: when Enobarbus tells Agrippa of Mark Antony's first sighting of Cleopatra ('Antony and Cleopatra', Act 2 Scene 2): 'For her own person, it beggar'd all description.' That is how John feels when he describes his vision of Jesus in Revelation 1.

Here is *beauty*: the long robe and gold belt (v.13), feet like bronze (v.15), his shining face (v.16). The old chorus says, 'Let the beauty of Jesus be seen in me.' And such *light*: the white head and hair and eyes like fire, his face like the shining sun. Talk of the darkness of sin and suffering, and 'in earth's darkest place, let there be light'. Here is *purity*: 'White as snow . . . blazing fire' (v.14), cleansing. Our soiled lives can be cleaned up. Overall, here is *power*: the eyes (v.14), his voice (v.15), the double-edged sword (v.16). If only this beauty, light, purity and power could be in us! Invite people to meet Jesus, to let these happen for them.

If you have time, talk about what Jesus is shown to do in this passage. Mention briefly how he shows us God (v.5, 'the faithful witness'), comparing 'the First and the Last' of verse 17 with verse 8. Especially at Easter, 'The first-born from the dead' (v.5) is appropriate, as is 'the ruler' (v.5) and 'he is coming' (v.7) for Ascension (with Revelation 22:20).

To make this great passage bring a great response, end with verses 5 and 6. We need to know that 'he loves us': enthuse about how special is the crucified and risen love of Christ. More than that, he 'has freed us from our sins by his blood' (echoes of 1 John 1:7). Ask who knows this in their lives now. We then become 'a kingdom and priests to serve his God and Father'. Briefly say how that affects you, leading to a call to meet and trust this risen, reigning Lord Jesus today.

14.7 Coming Soon—Jesus!

Bible references: Matthew 24:7, 30–51; Mark 9:47–48; Luke 16:26; John 3:36; 5:40; 14:2–3; Acts 1:11; Romans 13:11; 1 Corinthians 15:52; 1 Thessalonians 4:16–17; 2 Thessalonians 1:8–9; 2 Timothy 3:4–5; 2 Peter 3:3, 9–12; Revelation 20:14–15; 21:1–5; 22:7, 12, 20.

Audience: Advent and Ascension congregations.

Aim: To show the reality of Jesus' return, and our need to be ready.

Handy hint: There is a *lot* of material here. Be selective, but try not to miss the major points.

Outline: 'Just the facts, man!' Where are we heading? Where is the world going? With questions like this, say the one fact of which you are sure is that the world is heading to the return of Jesus. For every time the New Testament mentions the first coming, it talks of the second coming eight times more: on average once every twenty-five verses.

Jesus said he was returning (John 14:2–3, Matthew 24:30). The angels confirmed it (Acts 1:11), while Paul (1 Thessalonians 4:16, 1 Corinthians 15:52) and Peter (2 Peter 3:10) describe what it will be like. You could pick a few features, and even say that we don't have to believe it: he will come whether we believe it or not!

When? 'Soon' says the last chapter three times (Revelation 22:7, 12, 20). Talk of looking for signs of the weather changing. There are also signs for Jesus' return. Key passages are Matthew 24: people leave God out (v.37), nations fight—not just armies—a phenomenon of recent days (v.7), famines and earthquakes (v.7); and 2 Timothy 3: people loving pleasure (v.4), being 'religious' (v.5). No one believes in this (2 Peter 3:3), but Romans 13:11 is true. Pick a few, to show how these things happen today. 'Soon' could mean just that.

Explain the division there will be: Matthew 24:40–41, Revelation 20:11 and 15, and the need to trust Christ (John 5:40), and speak of how Jesus has already come, and died, to get us on the safe side. This division will be permanent (Luke 16:26). Heaven is real (1 Thessalonians 4:16–17, Revelation 21:1–5; 22:5)—enthuse a little! So is hell (Revelation 20:14–15, 2 Thessalonians 1:8–9). Jesus says so (Matthew 24:51, Mark 9:47–48, John 3:36). The modern church may prevaricate, but that is what Jesus died to save us from.

Ask what we should do. Peter gave the answer (2 Peter 3:11–12) to Christians, as did Jesus (Matthew 24:42). The main thing is to be ready (Matthew 24:44), by trusting him now. 2 Peter 3:9 shows his love in giving us today. Call for a response: nothing is more important, or urgent.

14.8 Power!

Bible reading: Isaiah 44. Also Psalm 42:1–2.

Audience: Pentecost season; Trinity Sunday.

Aim: To use a chapter of Isaiah to speak of the power of God, in particular the Holy Spirit, but combining the three Persons of the Trinity.

Handy hint: If the reading is too long, select the parts you will use and read those.

Outline: Start by talking about power-crazy people in a power-mad world. Say how we rely today on all sorts of things apart from God. Give current examples: the lottery's power to enrich, sexual prowess to attract, media power. God is not impressed with false gods, which is what these are (Isaiah 44:9–20). Show how powerless we seem to be over sin, the past, death, self. There is only one God (v.6). Let's look at his power!

You may want to touch on this briefly, but Isaiah mentions God's original and continuing power of creation (v.24). Unlike astrologers (and politicians), God predicts—and it happens (vv.7–8, also vv.27–28). The Father has power!

Don't you love verse 22? Introduce the power of Jesus,

as he has bought, and brought, forgiveness. The value of Isaiah 44 is that, in speaking of the Holy Spirit, you can include Father and Son also. Ask your audience if verse 22 has come true for them. If not—then today is their day.

At Pentecost, you will want to major on the power of the Holy Spirit. Verse 3 is one of the greatest Old Testament references. What a terrific picture! Try and paint with words the first half of the verse, and to explain the second half. Show how we are thirsty. You could bring in the beautiful Psalm 42:1–2. Share the result of letting God's Spirit fill us and change us (v.4). We become God's people (v.5). There is a wealth in the language: the way we are constantly watered by the 'streams'; the loveliness of 'poplars'.

Help your audience to feel their thirst. Take them to the thirst-quencher, and let him satisfy them!

14.9 The Greatest Contrast in the World

Bible passage: Romans 8:1–17. Also Proverbs 16:25; Isaiah 64:6; Matthew 7:21; John 6:28–29; 8:36; 14:16–17, 23; 2 Corinthians 5:17; Ephesians 5:18; Colossians 1:27.

Audience: Pentecost Sunday congregation.

Aim: To show the gulf between knowing and not knowing the Holy Spirit.

Handy hint: There is a lot of material here—prune as necessary.

Outline: This talk draws on Romans 8:1–17, one of the greatest passages in the Bible, and if you can't speak on this . . . !

Explain how the Bible is a book of contrasts, and you are going to talk about the greatest one. To be a Christian means to be 'in Christ Jesus' (v.1): Paul's favourite term (used 164 times by him, eg 2 Corinthians 5:17). Ask if that is where people are. Now turn it round. Where is God? Verse 9 is about the Spirit (see John 14:16–17); verse 10 about Jesus (as Colossians 1:27); verse 11 about the Father (also John 14:23). Is God in you?

Now the contrast. Show that there is our life, and God's

214

life. When we live without God we cannot please him (v.8 and Isaiah 64:6). We do not belong to Christ (v.9, and contrast Matthew 7:21 with John 6:28–29). This way leads to death (v.13, and Proverbs 16:25). Julian Charley said, 'Take seriously the biblical description of those without Christ.'

Welcome the good news! 'In Christ' we come alive (vv. 10–11) with the Spirit's witness (vv. 15–16). Show the difference this makes to you, and the honour of being one of God's children, and an heir (vv. 14–15 and 17). Speak of the amazing verse 1, 'No condemnation', and being 'set free' (v.2, also John 8:36) through the death and resurrection of Jesus.

Admit that this life has two sides: the joy of walking in the Spirit (v.4) and being led by him (v.14), and the hardships of verse 17.

Who will 'be filled with the Spirit' (Ephesians 5:18)? Today is the day to move from the dark to the light contrast. Invite your audience to receive God's Spirit now.

14.10 Too Late

Bible readings: Amos 8:1–12; John 15:1–11. Also Deuteronomy 30:15; Joshua 24:15; Psalm 95:7–8; Proverbs 29:1; Isaiah 1:18; Jeremiah 8:20; Mark 1:15; Acts 17:30; 2 Corinthians 6:2; Galatians 5:22–23; Hebrews 2:3; Revelation 22:17.

Audience: Harvest congregations.

Aim: To speak of the urgency of responding to Christ.

Visual aid: A basket of fruit, with an apple with a label showing its origin/type, a peach (stone removed, held together with cling film), a satsuma, a bunch of grapes.

Handy hint: The Amos reading is strong stuff! If you feel it is too 'heavy', use the John 15 reading only.

Outline: A simple quoting of Jeremiah 8:20 is a dramatic opening. And/or you could say you have brought your harvest offering, and produce the basket. Talk about a great and scary couple of verses: Amos 8:1–2. There is a pun in the Hebrew: two words, spelt differently but each pronounced 'kates', meaning 'a basket of fruit' and 'the end'. The NIV captures this: see the double use of 'ripe'. Good and bad news.

First, the good: your basket of fruit. What does God offer? The apple has a label on. Use it as a picture of God's forgiveness, which comes with a label—a cross. Speak of the love and sacrifice of Jesus. The peach, dramatically opened to reveal no stone, pictures the resurrection life (the stone of the grave has gone as well!). The satsuma is to be peeled, to show lots of fruit in one wrapping. Whizz through Galatians 5:22–23, and the fruit of the Spirit. The grapes take you to John 15:1–11, as we grow to produce fruit as part of Jesus, and part of each other in the church.

Now, the bad news. Amos 8, the second half of verse 2, leading to verse 11. Harvest is the end of the season: miss the fruit, and it is gone. If you did not start with Jeremiah 8:20, it fits here. Proverbs 29:1 and Hebrews 2:3 are key verses. Who dares say these things? We are scared of offending congregations: do we hold back the truth because of this?

The whole Bible says, 'Come now.' You could show this to build your own call: Deuteronomy 30:15 (The Pentateuch); Joshua 24:15 (The Histories); Psalm 95:7–8 (The Psalms); Isaiah 1:18 (The Prophets); Mark 1:15 (Jesus, The Gospels); Acts 17:30 (Acts); 2 Corinthians 6:2 (The Epistles); Revelation 22:17 (the last chapter). End with the basket: so much on offer; don't miss it.

15. A Little Law

Because the writer is himself a lawyer of over thirty years' standing, here are some suggestions for those situations where a little proof is needed for the Christian message. Christianity is true, and Jesus was right in saying, 'I am the Truth' (John 14:6). However, not everyone agrees!

These outlines will help where a reasoned presentation of the evidence will be a valuable tool in getting the message across.

15.1 Life Before Death

Bible reading: Luke 10:25–37. Also Mark 12:28–31; Luke 15:3–7; John 17:3.

Audience: Lawyers; business people; the good and the great.

Aim: To show that only in Jesus is there eternal life.

Outline: If you are a lawyer, or speaking where some are present, lament their bad image—not helped by the incident you are about to relate! Say how lawyers ask big questions, but never one bigger than Luke 10:25. Say why it is so vital to have a life which will not fade, or devalue. You could refer to the trivia of much modern-day living. What are we working for?

Here is a lawyer who asks the right questions, but gets the wrong answers. His reply to Jesus (v.27) is correct (see Jesus' own response in Mark 12:28–31), but impossible. He makes no further reference to loving God perfectly—he has failed that one. Leading with his chin, verse 29 invites a second realisation of failure.

As you deal with the story of the good Samaritan, notice that its primary purpose is to show the lawyer that he is *not* a good neighbour, thus failing both criteria for what

Jesus offers in verse 28. Show how much the Samaritan gave—courage, help, possessions, comfort, money—only to be a 'neighbour' (v.36). Verse 37 is impossible! Whoever succeeded in being that good?

Now to your point. Within five chapters Jesus would picture himself as the one who came looking in the right way (Luke 15:3–7). *He* is the good Samaritan. He comes with the wine of his blood and the oil of his Holy Spirit (v.34), riding on a donkey. He lifts us—but stays with us (unlike v.35). Draw in the importance of John 17:3, and how you have come to know God through Jesus.

Jesus proves that only he can give eternal life. Don't forget to emphasise that that was why he died, and that, alive from the dead, he now offers it to each one. Who will receive?

15.2 In God We Trust

Bible passage: Romans 4:1–8, 18–25. Also refer to Genesis 12:1–8; Psalm 51; Isaiah 41:8; Romans 10:9–10.

Audience: Church congregations; 'religious' people.

Aim: To show that everyone needs to trust their lives to God in order to be right with him.

Handy hint: In dealing with great biblical people, earth the talk in to your audience so they realise the personal application.

Outline: Some talks start best with a question: this is one of them! 'How can I be right with God?' or 'How can I know it's OK between me and God?' is what you are aiming for. Show why it is such a vital question: our eternity depends on the answer.

You might like to review Romans 10:9–10 as the basis for what you plan to prove. Or state that you believe that we need to put our whole trust in God: now you will explain why. Talk about what a clever man Paul was, and how his education would have included learning to think as a lawyer. He wants to encourage his readers in Rome to trust God. Why should they? How will he prove it?

Because the *best* person did. Coming out of Judaism, as

Christianity did, the great hero was still Abraham: he was the best, God's friend (Isaiah 41:8). Paul picks up Genesis 12:1–8 in Romans 4:13. The best trusted God. 'Are you the best?' you can ask. 'So? Do you trust God?'

We trust because the *worst* did. Who? King David. Show how he should have been the best (the Psalms, God's choice as king), but he sinned dreadfully regarding Bathsheba. Instead of bluffing it out, show his prayer in verses 7 and 8. Ask who is the worst person present (no one will volunteer!)—they can still trust God.

Get to the vital last two verses of the chapter, to show *where* our trust is to be: in God (v.24), in the death and resurrection of Jesus (vv.24–25), ie not in a system, creed, or in what we do. You could go back to the two men to show *how* we trust: humbly like David (you could mention bits of Psalm 51); bravely like Abraham (back to Genesis 12).

Best, worst, or somewhere in-between: who will join you in saying, 'In God we trust'?

15.3 Conclusive Evidence

Bible references: Luke 24:13–35; John 20; Acts 17:18; 1 Corinthians 15:1–11.

Audience: Intellectuals; those who would like to believe Christianity is true; Christians who want a foundation for their faith.

Aim: To prove the resurrection, the keystone to the truth of the Christian faith.

Visual aid: Why not borrow a wig and gown from a friendly barrister?!

Handy hint: Give the talk a good title in the pre-meeting publicity (eg 'Dead men don't rise').

Caution: There is a *lot* of evidence for the resurrection: this talk could last for hours!

Outline: You could divide the evidence for the resurrection into two: what happened at the time, and the history of Christianity to the present day. Don't panic if you mention some points briefly and major on others.

Contemporary events

(1) Many witnesses. Four or five witnesses suffice in most cases: over 500 saw Jesus alive. Paul is good on this in 1 Corinthians 15. Describe the sort of non-gullible folk they were—good women, fishermen used to 'you-should-have-seen-the-one-that-got-away', doubting Thomas, people who died for it.

(2) The number of sightings: at least eleven, often for a long time. You could describe the Emmaus walk (Luke 24:13–35), or the Thomas incidents in John 20. This links with:

(3) The different writers: nine in the New Testament, plus Josephus (Jew), Tacitus (Roman) and others.

(4) The alternatives are impossible. If Jesus was not really dead, how did he recover so miraculously from all he suffered? If he did not rise, who took the body? The disciples—who died for a lie? The Jews, or the Romans—who then let the disciples challenge their lives? Body snatchers—who left the clothes?

Consequent effects

(1) The history of Christianity is not 'Follow these teachings' but 'Jesus and the resurrection' (Acts 17:18). Give a couple of illustrations of great people in history who knew the risen Jesus personally (Augustine, C.S. Lewis, Jonathan Edwards).

(2) Take off your barrister's wig, pretend to go to the witness box, and be the final witness. 'I know the resurrection is real because I have met the risen Jesus: he is my personal Saviour.' Speak briefly of the truth of this.

You could end with, 'Members of the Jury, what is your verdict?' Add, as a PS, 'So?'

15.4 Don't Do It!

Bible passage: John 8:2–11. Also Luke 19:10; Colossians 1:19–23.

Audience: Church services; ladies; prisons; lawyers.

Aim: To prove that we are in danger of misreading Jesus, thinking he is hard and judgemental, and missing his forgiveness.

Handy hint: You will need to angle this talk according to your audience. The more their realisation of their own shortcomings (eg those in prison) the more gentle you should be—and vice versa!

Outline: If you were into earthy music, an introduction which includes Ian Dury's 'Sex and drugs and rock'n'roll' would go well in certain circumstances, particularly if you can admit to two out of three (don't say which!). Sex is not an invention of the last fifty years, and adultery was prevalent when Jesus was here: so there are three things not to do (surprise people with what they are, because they think you are going to talk about not being naughty!).

Don't *mislead* Jesus. Follow John 8:2–11 as the incident unfolds. Many are guilty of misusing sex: *all* are guilty of some sin (Colossians 1:21). Who is perfect (v.7)? They

226

tried to mislead Jesus, and failed. There is no room for
goody-goodies, pointing self-righteous fingers.

Secondly, don't *misjudge* Jesus (a good one for a talk to
lawyers!). Show what a wicked demand was made in
verses 5 and 6. It was a 'no win' situation. 'Stone her'
was against Roman law (only Rome could condemn to
death). 'Don't' was against Jewish law. The leaders had
no idea who Jesus was, or why he had come: you could
refer to Colossians 1:20 and Luke 19:10. He is not going
to 'condemn' (v.11)—he is going to take the condemnation. Explain his death, including taking our (and the
woman's) shame.

Say that, with such love, we must not *miss* Jesus. The
tragedy is not the woman, but those who went away (v.9).
We can be right with God (Colossians 1:22): which will
mean, by the way, no adultery (Colossians 1:23)—so
'Don't do it' did mean that, after all!

Emphasise the positive, as you end. Jesus is terrific—he
forgives, welcomes, pays for our wrong, gives new life.
Someone said, 'Dear God, help me to get up. I can fall
down by myself!' Missing Jesus? Don't do it!

15.5 Conclusions

Bible references: Romans 1:29–32; 2:1; 3:22–23; 5:1, 8–9; 7:18–19; 8:1–2; 12:1–2.

Audience: Churchgoers; those with some Bible knowledge.

Aim: To prove the need for a Holy Spirit encounter, to enable Jesus to make us as God wants us to be.

Handy hint: Alternative titles could be 'Therefore!' or 'You can be sure of this!'. The talk is a walk through Romans. Don't be ashamed of holding a Bible/New Testament open, and quoting extensively: let God's word do the work!

Outline: Start with 'No one ever wrote a letter with verses', to explain that Paul did not divide up Romans. When you were at school, you ended essays/maths problems with 'Therefore . . .', to prove your point. Here is a weird discovery: a quarter of the letter to the Romans has chapters with 'Therefore' at the start! Each proves a point.

Chapter 2:1: 'Therefore . . . no excuse.' For what? For pretending to be innocent of wrongdoing. You could give a quick run through 1: 29–32, saying how several do apply to you, even if some do not. Or you could go on to 3:22–

228

23, or 7:18–19. Say that it is 'honesty spot' time: we are guilty as charged.

Which makes the next 'Therefore' quite amazing (5:1). Take your audience into 5:8–9, and speak of the greatness of the death of Christ on the cross, dealing with our guilt. Flick on to 8:1, for the third 'Therefore', showing the new life of the Holy Spirit in 8:2. Share from your own experience how vital these three 'Therefores' are, and how your own life has been changed by them.

All this leads to the conclusion that we had better do something. Romans 12:1 is the answer. J.B. Phillips' tremendous 12:2 follows: 'Don't let the world around you squeeze you into its own mould, but let God re-mould your minds from within, so that you may prove in practice that the plan of God for you is good, meets all his demands and moves towards the goal of true maturity.'

Has Paul proved the case? Then invite a heart as well as a head response, using Romans 12:1.

16. Acceptable Appeals

Sometimes it is appropriate to invite people to make an open, public response to the call of Christ. Unfortunately this has fallen into disrepute because of its being done badly. How can there be a call to 'stand up and be counted' in a responsible way?

Further help on this difficult and controversial subject will be found in Part One. Here are four outlines which can be used in making an open appeal.

16.1 Election Day

Bible references: Joshua 24:15; Matthew 6:24; 25:41; 27:39–44; Mark 15:12 (a Bible reading could be Mark 15:1–15); Luke 23:42.

Audience: Those at the end of a period of faith-sharing, when an open call is appropriate; Christmas and Holy Week congregations.

Aim: To show that there are a limited number of responses to Jesus, and everyone makes one or another.

Handy hint: The Outline deals with people's reactions to the crucifixion. However, it can be easily adapted for Christmas. The alternatives are added each time in brackets (C).

Outline: Make-your-mind-up time/elections/time to vote. Find a recent/impending event where decisions are made, and explain that it is the same with Jesus. Or say that you have been sharing the manifesto of Jesus, now it is time to decide (Mark 15:12).

You could give a brief résumé of what Jesus offers: forgiveness of sins, new life, the Holy Spirit, heaven—and a call to total commitment, with the challenge that entails. What will we do? Our choices are limited, as at any election. We can do as people did when Jesus was crucified (C. born).

We can vote against: the crowd shouted 'Crucify him!' (C. Herod the king wanted the baby killed.) Suggest reasons why people do (don't believe, don't need/want Jesus, it's too hard). We must accept the consequences: we get the opposition party (Matthew 25:41).

We can do nothing: many do not vote at elections. Pilate tried to do that, washing his hands. (C. The townsfolk of Bethlehem missed what was going on.) History says 'Crucified under Pontius Pilate.' Abstaining lets in the opposition: it is a 'No' vote. As is voting both ways: Simon Peter. (C. The inn-keeper—let Jesus in, but only to the cowshed.) See Matthew 6:24, and recall Peter's tears: one side or the other. Fooling around, laughing (Matthew 27:39–44), and the dice-throwing soldiers send Jesus to the cross. (C. This is today's trivialisation of Christmas.) The election is on, whatever we do.

As quickly as possible, get to a 'Yes' vote: the thief on the cross (Luke 23:42), or you could use Joseph of Arimathea. (C. Joseph, the Wise Men.) Whatever others said, the thief and Joseph were for Jesus. Are we? Who will give an unequivocal 'Yes' today? Then do it!

16.2 Limping

Bible passage: 1 Kings 18:17–39. Also 2 Corinthians 6:2.

Audience: Those who have heard the message before, and now need to make a real step of faith.

Aim: To encourage a very positive response to Jesus Christ, using a great Old Testament incident in 1 Kings 18.

Handy hint: Throughout the talk, make it clear that God challenges us to make an open, positive response to his call to own him as our God. Then your call at the end will come as an obvious conclusion.

Make sure you know the background to the incident.

Outline: Thumb-nail sketch 'the story so far': evil Ahab, the people following false gods, Elijah as God's man, and the challenge of verse 21. Some versions put it: 'How long will you go on limping between two opinions?' which is a good picture of their attitude. It is showdown time—then, and now.

In those days it was gods of wood and stone versus God. Describe some of today's sophisticated gods—more subtle, but just as real: money, possessions, horoscopes. Make them relevant to your audience. On the other hand:

Jesus, Name above all names,
Beautiful Saviour, Glorious Lord,
Emmanuel, God is with us,
Blesséd Redeemer, Living Word.

Nadia Hearn. Copyright ©
Scripture in Song/Thankyou
Music 1974, 1979. Used by permission.

A run through these descriptions of Jesus will build a composite picture of the 'King of kings and Lord of lords'. Speak of how special these names are to you, as Jesus means 'God with us', he saves and redeems us (buying us back), and he is the living God, bringing new life.

You can talk about the challenge of Elijah, as the people finally made their open and verbal response in verse 39. As Jesus hangs on the cross, comes from the tomb, stands here now: what is our choice? It was dramatic, and you can make it so now. Let God's Spirit give you the style, as well as the words.

Call people out to the joy of owning Jesus as Lord—no more 'limping'. Today's the day (2 Corinthians 6:2).

16.3 Just as I Am

Bible passage: John 6:25–40. Also John 1:29.

Audience: A service where 'Just as I am' will be sung after the talk, as a definite call to respond to Christ is given.

Aim: To encourage a positive, open commitment to Jesus Christ.

Handy hint: The hymn could be on sheets, or overhead projector, to concentrate attention.

Outline: As the whole talk is a walk through the hymn 'Just as I am, without one plea', you could mention what a great hymn it is, and how you are using it because Charlotte Elliott said what you want to say: except she did it in 1834!

Say that you want to explain how people become Christians, and how we come personally ('Just as *I* am'). You could introduce your own story at once—how a friend/parent was already a Christian, but you had to come yourself. Agree the shock of 'without one plea', and show how we could never be good enough. Jesus gives a great answer in John 6:28–29.

Make a big thing of God's answer in Jesus: 'But that thy

blood was shed for me.' You may need to explain why
Jesus is called the 'Lamb of God' at the end of each verse:
recall John 1:29.

Now make the call, so people are ready to respond at the
end: 'I *come*.' You could show how the verb is personal,
positive (definite, open, clear) and present tense. Who will
come? The rest of the hymn will give you scope to pick up
the barriers we pass through as we come. There may be
'many a conflict, many a doubt'. Show how you still
struggle, and understand so little. But you have come,
and find that Jesus has the answers. 'Fighting and fears'
will let you admit how scared you are—and that Jesus
understands. We may feel unworthy, 'poor, wretched,
blind', with verse 35 helping here.

Enthuse about Jesus' reaction: he welcomes us (v.37).
Don't miss the sense of full commitment: 'Thine alone.'

So: 'Lamb of God—I *come*.' Let's do it!

16.4 Help!

Bible passage: Matthew 14:22–34.

Audience: Church congregations, or large groups where an open call is appropriate; young people.

Aim: To call people to a definite, positive response to Christ.

Handy hint: This is an exciting adventure, with some real humour. Make it live.

Outline: You might like to give a quick background to Peter's character. Or you could get straight into the incident with a brief, dramatic account of the feeding of the 5,000, and what happened afterwards (vv. 22–24). Or you could say how like Peter you are—good intentions which don't quite work out. Whichever, set the scene as if introducing a comic drama.

It is possible to admire Peter's courage, or deride his impetuosity; but as he is going to get it wrong, there is something to be said for praising the fact that he *did* 'walk on water' (v.29). Preachers often lambast people's failures. God knows we sometimes get it right. You could give examples of where your hearers have done well.

Of course, it did go wrong. The opposition was too

strong (v.30, first half). Phillips' paraphrase has Jesus saying, in verse 31, 'You lost your nerve.' David Watson said, 'We face a crisis of powerlessness.' Show how you lose—as does everyone. If you want some humour, describe Peter's alternatives. 'I'm the only one to walk on water. I've done my best. On balance I'm better than the rest'—he has three seconds before his mouth reaches the water. Equate this to the way we try to bluff through with our 'goodness'. Or, Peter can say the three words in verse 30. Why won't we?

The same Jesus who saved him will save us. Speak of the nail-pierced hand, the love, the strength of Jesus. C.H. Spurgeon said: 'I have a great need for Christ. I have a great Christ for my need.' As you hope to call people to respond openly, major on the other disciples seeing every-thing—their amusement, telling everyone back home. But Peter was safe, and walked on water again, held by Jesus.

Verse 34 is good. Gennesaret was home; and Jesus will bring us safe home to heaven. People may have smiled at Peter's failure, but they would go to him later to find how Jesus could help them, too.

Now invite those who want to know the safe grip of Jesus to come—even 'tough' men, 'good' people, and other categories you will have mentioned as you applied the talk.

17. New Life

The response to the call to trust Christ is vital. However, it is but one step in the process of knowing Jesus Christ as Lord. What about those who do respond? This section contains ways of helping such people.

17.1 Baby Christians: Day 1

Bible references: Galatians 2:20; Philippians 4:6; Hebrews 5:12; 1 Peter 2:2; 1 John 1:9.

Audience: Brand-new Christians, in a group or one-to-one; counsellors.

Aim: To encourage new Christians to get through the first day or two of their new life in Christ. To help those counselling to have a simple outline to guide new Christians in their first steps forward.

Visual aid: If possible, hold a real baby (parent present for emergencies). Your audience would remember the talk for ever!

Handy hints: Be easy to understand. Encourage. Don't be heavy. Remember: 'New life—handle with care.'

Outline: Start with a 'new baby' story from your experience—happy, funny, positive. Babies are great: but what do they do? Because a new Christian is a baby for God, however old they are physically, you can draw helpful parallels.

Babies cry! It proves they are alive. Good parents understand what is meant by the cry. So we cry out to

242

God in prayer, about anything and everything (Philippians 4:6). Tell them how prayer helps you, and how God hears and answers.

Babies feed. Use 1 Peter 2:2, and point them in the direction of Mark's Gospel, or Luke, as a starter. Encourage the use of notes for guidance. 'Solid food' (Hebrews 5:12) will follow!

Bring an element of surprise as you mention the fact that *babies also make a mess*! Christians are not perfect, and a new Christian must not panic when things seem to go wrong. God has a clean-up system in 1 John 1:9.

Most of all, *babies enjoy love*. Describe God's love for his children (Galatians 2:20), and how he has promised never to let us go. From this will flow our love for him, and our sharing him with others. But right now, at the beginning, the best thing about being a new Christian is enjoying a Father's love and care, and that of the Christian family, too.

You could conclude with a prayer for the new Christians, with a feel-good factor in it.

17.2 My Greatest Ambition

Bible passage: Philippians 3:7–16. Also 1 Corinthians 15:57.

Audience: Primarily for Christians; can also work evangelistically.

Aim: To work through Philippians 3:10 to explain what a real Christian is, and the impact that has on life.

Handy hint: It is worth checking the various nuances of several translations: the Authorised and Amplified Versions are particularly helpful—and even the Latin Vulgate! (Don't panic, the Outline has the bit you need from that . . . .)

Outline: Ask for a bit of audience participation, to discover a few burning ambitions (a favourite team to win the Cup, a holiday in Tahiti, to live in a mansion). Or suggest a few outrageous ones yourself. Talk of great people, and how Christianity has its heroes. One of the best was Paul. Give a summary of his achievements: he lists some in Philippians 3:4–6. How did he view them? Speak of his dramatic conclusion in verse 7 and the first half of verse 8: the Amplified has 'mere rubbish'. Show his reason in part two of verse 8 and verse 9.

Now here is Paul's ambition in verse 10, 'I want to know Christ.' Have you got a good story of a famous person everyone knows *about*, but you (or a family member) have met personally? This will help you contrast knowing about Jesus and a personal relationship with him. Could you speak of your own experience when you knew lots about Christianity, but needed that encounter with Jesus? Share the great difference, now you and he have got together.

For Paul, and you and your hearers, it means two things. First, 'the power of his resurrection'. You could talk dramatically of what happened on Easter morning: all that power brought to our lives, and its victory (1 Corinthians 15:57). Ask if the Holy Spirit is being allowed to make this happen. Then, secondly, in the rest of the verse: the Latin Vulgate literally translates as 'the communion of his passion'. As Jesus longs for the world to come to him, we will look with his eyes and ache with his heart. And why? Verse 11 wraps it up.

'Who will be a Christian like that?' you could ask.

17.3 To Be Sure!

Bible reading: 1 John 5:9–13. Also John 14:19; Romans 8:16.

Audience: Those unsure about their relationship with God.

Aim: To bring assurance of salvation. This is a gentle walk through 1 John 5:9–13.

Handy hint: This talk could lead to a real release for some listeners. Give time at the end for prayer and quiet response.

Outline: An Irish accent helps if you plan to start with 'To be sure!' The Irish are always saying it. Wouldn't it be great 'to be sure' we really are Christians? Here is some help from a letter by one of Jesus' closest friends, John. Why not read the verses here?

Do you have a story of someone saying something like, 'I've been coming to church for fifty years, but I'm not really sure I'm a Christian/going to heaven'? Admit to your own doubts (or ones you have had in the past). How can we find an answer?

First, eternal life is from God, not us (v.11). Because it is a gift, it cannot be earned. Give a couple of examples of how people try to earn the gift, eg 'I do my best,' 'I'm a leader in the church.' But it is Jesus who brings us eternal life (v.11). Speak of his life, and his death as our substitute (a 'sub' is one who plays in another's place). Recall his resurrection and his words in John 14:19, and sending the Holy Spirit.

Therefore, secondly, with Jesus comes life (v.12 part 1). Has Jesus come to your life? John Wesley wrote: 'Only the power that made the world can make a Christian.' The second half of verse 12 must also be true. Dr James Kennedy said, 'The reason so many people today do not know whether they are on their way to heaven is that they are not on their way to heaven.'

Thirdly, if we trust Jesus, we will be sure (v.13). Romans 8:16 could be introduced here. Robert Murray McCheyne wrote to a friend, 'I seem to know Jesus Christ better than any of my earthly relatives.'

Why not conclude with a word of how you found all this came true for you when . . . ? You could offer to pray with and for those who are seeking to be sure.

17.4 Potty

Bible reading (in the order used): Jeremiah 18:1–6; 2 Kings 4:1–7; John 7:37–44; Jeremiah 2:13. Also Luke 11:13.

Audience: Christians; can be used to explain what Christians are to those who want to come in.

Aim: To speak of pottery, fullness and emptiness, showing how God will fill our lives.

Visual aid: If you could get a potter with a wheel to throw a pot before or during the talk, it would be remembered by the audience for ever.

Handy hint: Each incident is a good story: be a good story-teller, and the talk will flow.

Outline: Are Christians 'potty'? Barry Maguire was asked, in a radio interview; 'Aren't all you Christians brainwashed?' 'Everyone is,' he replied. 'We just chose who washed our brains.'

Potty? Take your audience, in their minds' eye, with Jeremiah to the potter (Jeremiah 18:1–6). We are all 'marred', needing to be re-made. Shirley Williams said, 'People hunger for a new beginning.' Say how you put your life in the scarred hands of Jesus, and how he is re-forming your life.

Then to story two: 2 Kings 4:1–7. Again, enter into the story, and relate it to John 7:37–44, as Jesus offers his Spirit to fill our lives. David Watson said, 'The greatest need of today is a spiritual renewal. Both individual Christians and whole churches need to be continually filled with the Spirit.' You might want to speak of us being the ones who set the limits: the last jar meant no more oil (2 Kings 4:6).

You will have to decide whether to leave it there, or to bring in the tragedy of Jeremiah 2:13, and its implied warning for us. But don't end on a negative. You can end with the John 7 passage, or Luke 11:13. Encourage and enthuse a response to God's generosity.

17.5 This Is Christianity!

Bible references: Ezekiel 37:1–14 (would make a good reading); Psalm 16:11; Isaiah 26:3; 65:14; Ezekiel 33:11; Luke 15:7; John 1:4; 3:16; 10:10, 28; 11:25–26; 14:6, 27; 15:11; 16:33; 17:3; Romans 6:23; 15:33; Ephesians 2:14–17; Philippians 4:7; Colossians 3:15; Hebrews 12:2; James 1:2; Jude 24.

Audience: Christians; anyone with whom you wish to speak about some of the basic characteristics of Christianity.

Aim: To take three key words which the Bible uses to explain the Christian faith.

Handy hint: There are other words! This Outline may give clues how to build a talk around one or two words. Each of the three words may contain enough material for a talk: a fourth could be 'love' (and on to 'power', 'certainty' . . .).

Outline: Explain that you want to bring the good news of God's promises for Christians, using three great words. (Martin Luther said, 'Every promise of God is made to me.')

The first word is *joy*. Pick your favourites from John 15:11, Psalm 16:11 and Isaiah 65:14 to show that Christians are allowed to be happy! Jesus went via the cross for this joy (Hebrews 12:2), and heaven rejoices when we come (Luke 15:7). It is even good to suffer (James 1:2)—a wry comment on this, perhaps? Even death means joy (Jude 24).

The next word is *peace*. You might say that joy is for good times, and peace is for the rest of life! Jesus gives this (John 14:27). It is too good for words (Philippians 4:7). It is for tough days (John 16:33). God is the God of peace (Romans 15:33), but he must be in charge (Colossians 3:15, and the lovely Isaiah 26:3). Peace is because Jesus died, whether we are near or far (Ephesians 2:14–17). There is a lot here: pick your favourite bits, and enthuse over them!

The third word is *life*. Here are some more seed thoughts. You do not have to quote each reference, but convey the essence. More than anything else, Jesus brings life (John 10:10, 28). Knowing him is life (John 17:3). He is that life (John 1:4, 11:25–26; 14:6). It cost him everything (John 3:16), so he gives it freely (Romans 6:23). The corollary is that God does not want us to die (Ezekiel 33:11).

If you have not read Ezekiel 37:1–14 yet, here is a surprise place for the reading, and a great passage with which to end. Antoine de Saint-Exupéry said in his *Wind, Sand and Stars*, 'Only the Spirit, if he breathe into the clay, can create Man.' If your audience needs to trust Christ, invite them to receive the Spirit's breath.

17.6 Mr Nice Guy

Bible references: Acts 4:36–37; 9:26–27; 11:19–30; 13:2, 50; 15:37, 39. If preached, the Acts 11 passage is a good Bible reading.

Audience: Christians, new and old, and those who want to see what being one entails.

Aim: To portray Barnabas as an example for us to follow as a real Christian.

Handy hint: Try to really enter in to the character, making him a real, warm person, not just a figure of history.

Outline: Introduce yourself as not-the-most-brilliant Christian (unless you are. If so, please contact the author of this book: he'd be honoured to meet you). Say how you have found the person you would most like to be like when you grow up! Name: Barnabas—one of the first followers of Jesus in Acts. He is Mr Nice Guy. Simply pick out your favourite bits of his life and speak of them, showing how God's Holy Spirit can change us to be like that. Here are a few of his characteristics:

He *gave*. That is the first thing Acts tells us about Barnabas (4:36–37). Share how much Jesus has given us (forgiveness through the cross, new life, his Spirit, heaven), which motivates you (or, you know it should) to give.

He *befriended*. The disciples were suspicious of Paul's conversion, but Barnabas reacted differently (9:26–27). Similarly, when John Mark got the brush-off, Barnabas stuck with him (15:37, 39). You might want to bring in here the meaning of his name (4:36), and how Jesus himself encourages you.

Barnabas was *happy* (11:23). A little levity about how Christians are allowed to smile! He *helped* (11:26). Is that why we are now all 'Christians'? He *worked* (13:2) as God called him. He *endured* suffering (13:50). These latter three features are worth a mention, and you may want to say how people like that are still at a premium today.

Now—the secret: make a big thing of Acts 11:24. C.H. Spurgeon was a great Baptist preacher in London 150 years ago. His brother was asked the secret of C.H.'s success. 'I think it lies in the fact that he loves Jesus of Nazareth, and Jesus of Nazareth loves him.'

Conclude with something along the lines of: 'The world needed a Barnabas. It still does. Who will be one?'

17.7 Dead and Alive

Bible references: Galatians 2:20. Also Romans 5:8; 6:23; 1 Peter 3:18; Revelation 21:5.

Audience: New Christians; more mature Christians; seekers; at an adult baptism.

Aim: To show the total change of life Jesus brings, and to emphasise his love, using Galatians 2:20 as the basis.

Outline: Have a big opening statement, to show how enormous is the change which takes place when we become Christians. Not so much a reformation as a revolution. As your talk is based on Galatians 2:20, it might be good to quote it very early on.

Try to draw out the drama of Paul's 'I have been crucified with Christ', maybe talking about the degradation of crucifixion, as well as the finality of death. Why not show what a good idea it was to let the old, godless life die, because it was dead anyway (Romans 6:23)? That would lead you to the death of Jesus for us (1 Peter 3:18). By receiving what Jesus has done, the old has gone.

Welcome, new life—in Jesus. Take the rest of the verse except the final bit. Enthuse about Jesus being alive, back from the dead and the gift of the Holy Spirit: not just

beside to guide, but within to empower. Share how you
personally 'live by faith in the Son of God', and how
God's promise to 'make all things new' (Revelation
21:5) happens now, as well as when Jesus returns. Try
to get across the concept of a totally different life and
lifestyle.

Build to the verse's climax: 'Who loved me and gave
himself for me.' You may want to re-emphasise the love
shown on the cross (Romans 5:8). Encourage your hearers
to live in the wonder, bask in the sunshine and bathe in the
glory of that love.

17.8 Zerubbabel!

Bible references: Nehemiah 12:47; Ezra 2:2; 3:2; Haggai 1:1–6, 12–15; 2:1–5, 20–23; Zechariah 4:6–10; Matthew 1:12.

Audience: Christians of all ages; those new to the faith; those perhaps waning in enthusiasm.

Aim: To take a great Old Testament character, show how he got it right, and encourage others to take a leaf out of his book.

Visual aid: Smarties for the winners!

Handy hint: Make it fun! Even Zerubbabel's name rolls off the tongue well. He is an enthusiast for God—be one also in presentation style.

Outline: Joke about the way speakers often have three points, each beginning with the same letter. Here's a man with a wacky name—Zerubbabel—and here are three things about him, all starting with 'Z'! Can the audience guess them before you give them? No answers now, but a prize at the end for whoever (truthfully!) got them all.

As background, Zerubbabel's name means 'seed of Babylon' (not a very godly name)—check the two Ezra

256

references. He is in the lineage of Jesus (Matthew 1:12). Here are the three 'Z's:

Zerubbabel had *zap*. What made him great, and be zappy? Haggai gives the answers: God spoke to him (1:1 and 2:20). He responded (1:12), agreeing that he was like the rest. C.H. Spurgeon said, 'We are all aristocrats in our own righteousness; we do not like to bend down and come among common sinners.' Zerubbabel agreed he was part of the problem. So he let God change him (1:14). William Lane said, 'The Christian is never a self-made man.'

Secondly, Zerubbabel had *zeal* (that is the one they will guess!). He worked for God (Haggai 2:2–4, Nehemiah 12:47). Not many do. Christianity is like soccer—70,000 in the stands urgently in need of exercise, twenty-two on the pitch urgently in need of rest! He sees God work (2:21), and works with him. Haggai 2:23 is a great verse!

Finally, the *zest* of Zerubbabel (how he did it) is in Zechariah 4. It is God's power (v.6), God's grace (v.7), God's victory (v.10). Zerubbabel is great because God did it.

Who got all three? Who will *be* all three?

18. Look Out!

While we may be motivated in sharing our faith (hence our interest in this book), others may not feel the same enthusiasm. Here are three outlines to enable us to encourage our Christian friends and congregations to get going in their faith-sharing, too.

18.1 Men of Jesus

Bible passage: Matthew 9:35–38.

Audience: Christians who need to be inspired not only to share their faith, but to do it in the right way.

Aim: To show how Jesus shared the good news, as an inspiration for us today.

Outline: Say how it is great to be involved in proclaiming the Christian faith. To get it right, why not watch the master craftsman at work? It might be good to look at the reading here. If you like three points beginning with the same letter, here goes!

The *message* of Jesus is good news (v.35). You could talk about the bad news for people, worldwide, nationally and personally. A few examples from this week's news will make the talk particularly relevant. Speak of the hurts and problems individuals face, to show how vital the message of Jesus is. Pick out three or four features of Jesus which make his message good for you (forgiveness, joy, peace, friendship, Holy Spirit, heaven), giving a couple of applications.

But how to share the message? Consider the *method* of Jesus. Instead of being evangelistic first, he taught (all three points of 'method' are in verse 35). Allude to the ignorance of the nation, and how we have to explain even basic concepts. Only then can we preach, and call people. Don't leave out the healing aspect. Jesus reached the whole person, not just 'souls to be saved'.

Why was Jesus so special? Not just because of his message and method, but because of who he was, and is. For us today, we must be *men* and women of Jesus. Draw out the style of Jesus in verses 36 to 39, especially the word 'compassion'. How is our 'heart'? His tears for Jerusalem, and his 'passion' (what a word to describe the agony of the cross), should be reflected in us.

The challenge for our reaching out is all there in these few verses. Share them with the desire to motivate your hearers, and call them to respond with heart and action.

18.2 Who Needs Evangelism?

Bible references: Luke 4:18; John 8:34, 36; Acts 26:9–20; 1 John 5:19.

Audience: Christians; churches/groups wondering whether to do some evangelism and outreach.

Aim: To show to Christians the needs of those who are not yet Christians.

Visual aid: Find someone who could speak briefly of the change Jesus has made in their life, and how one or more of the examples below have had happened for them.

Handy hint: Have lots of illustrations of people who fit each category, quotes from the week's news, up-to-date statistics.

Outline: Paul was given a five-point plan for his work in Acts 26:18. His first task is '*to open their eyes*', following the work of Jesus (Luke 4:18). Describe the blindness of many to the gospel (eg a survey showed that a third of those asked in a recent opinion poll 'What is Easter?' did not know). We must share the truth, show God to people.

Secondly, '*Turn them from darkness to light*.' Many are in darkness, eg suffering, loneliness (Beatles 'All the

lonely people'), bereavement, broken homes and marriages. Life is purposeless, and people are lost. As the
prayer-book puts it, 'Lighten our darkness.' Show how
Jesus brings his light: it would help if you had an example
from your own life.

Next, Paul is to bring people *'from the power of Satan
to God'*. 1 John 5:19 is strong, as is John 8:34. Thank God
for John 8:36, as Jesus sets us free. Antoine de Saint-
Exupéry said in his *Wind, Sand and Stars*, 'We all yearn
to escape from prison.'

Now here are the two answers: first, *'That they may
receive forgiveness of sins.'* Talk about the centrality of
the cross. John Stott, in *Christian Mission in a Modern
World*, says, 'Forgiveness remains man's chief need, and
an indispensable part of the good news.' Share your joy at
sins forgiven.

The other half is, *'A place among those who are sanc-
tified by faith in me.'* Speak of the glory of a relationship
with God through Jesus: new life, new family, new Lord,
new holiness, heaven. Ishmael says in his song: 'Father
God, I wonder how I managed to exist without the knowledge of your parenthood and your loving care.'

Conclude with: 'How can we fail to go to these people?'

18.3 One at a Time

Bible passage: Luke 15:1–10.

Audience: Christians; also good in prison or with hurting people.

Aim: To encourage involvement in personal faith-sharing.

Handy hint: Make this talk as personal as possible, so each one feels involved. Have personal examples of people (you don't have to name or identify them) for whom *you* have a concern.

Outline: Get each one of your audience to think of three people: define the categories. If they can't get someone in the first group they need two in the second set. Without sitting in judgement, you want them to think of three people who may well not yet be Christians. Your categories could be: family/relations, friends/neighbours, work colleagues/ people they meet regularly.

Now for the thrust of the talk: you want to show how Jesus sees those people, so the viewpoint of your audience will become like his. Get to Luke 15:1–10.

All through, show the care and concern of Jesus. Refer to the criticism of verse 2: but Jesus prefers the word 'lost' (vv.4, 9). You could speak of that as being more loving, while not denying the 'sinner's' jibe, which he only brings in when the 'sinner' is back home (v.7). We have all been like that. When *The Times*' correspondence column was dealing with 'What's wrong with the world?', G.K. Chesterton wrote, 'Dear Sir, I am. Yours faithfully.' Give an example of someone (yourself?) being lost, and the joy of being found. Do we blame people, or see their lostness?

That concern leads to the value Jesus places on each person: ninety-nine left for one lost. If every family member/neighbour/friend were a Christian bar one, Jesus would look for that one. Do we? Say something about how much Jesus cares. He died for them, he paid with his life for the 'lost sheep'.

Finally, you could talk about what difference it will all make. The sheep is brought 'home', the coin is restored to the place of honour, heaven rejoices. How can we fail them by not sharing the good news? Suggest they pray for them every day, and look for openings to talk. Our faith is for giving away!

Thematic Index

Scripture Index

	Talk no.
Job	
15:14	12.4
19:25	2.5
23:10	3.1
Psalms	
8:4–5	2.6, 14.1
14:1	14.3
14:3	10.4
16:11	17.5
19:7–11	3.1
23	8.2
34:8	11.2
37:25	8.4
42:1–2	14.8
51	15.2
51:3	10.3
51:5	9.4
51:6	12.3
51:7	12.4
61:2	7.2
71:18	8.4
81	7.2
81:6	3.8
84:10	6.1
90:2	5.1
92:14	8.4
95:7–8	14.10
119:105	3.5
119:127	3.1
124	7.4
Proverbs	
3:5–6	3.5
12:15	14.3
14:9	14.3
16:25	14.9
21:2	12.3

	Talk no.
22:6	11.5
23:26	12.3
29:1	14.10
Ecclesiastes	
2:14	14.3
Isaiah	
1:18	12.4, 13.3, 14.10
1:5–6	13.3
6	9.4
6:3	5.3
6:5	12.4
6:8	10.3
7:14	2.3, 2.4
9:6	2.3
26:3	17.5
28:16	1.2
30:21	10.4
40:28	8.2
41:8	15.2
44	14.8
44:22	8.3, 12.4
46:4	8.4
49:15–16	1.1
49:16	11.5
52:13–53:10	9.1
52:14	2.6
53:3	14.3
53:5	5.1, 6.6
53:6	2.3, 10.4
55	4.4
55:1	9.1
55:6–7	10.4
55:8–9	2.6
59:2	10.3, 10.4
64:6	5.1, 9.4, 12.4, 14.9